Guide to the

CSJ UK | Camino

The Confraternity of Saint Jam... comprises three separate bookl...

- **Preparing for the Camino Francés**
- **Guide to the Camino Francés**
- **Pilgrim Guide to Santiago de Compostela**

The first may be left at home when you depart. The second will prove invaluable to you and other pilgrims on your pilgrimage. The third may be packed away safely in your pack until you get nearer to Santiago.

© Markus Selle

Introduction

This guide provides all of the information needed for pilgrims who wish to walk or cycle the *Camino Francés,* from Saint-Jean-Pied-de-Port on the French side of the Pyrenees to Santiago de Compostela in Galicia in the far north west of Spain. It is referred to throughout this guide simply as "the Camino".

General notes on the entries

Key to symbols used throughout the Guide

A	Albergues, gîtes d'étape, youth hostels
H	Other accommodation/cafés/shops
C	Campsites
PR	Private albergue which may take reservations as opposed to municipal, church or association-run albergues which generally do not
♦	Price per person for a bed, usually a bunk bed in a dormitory
♦ ♦	Price for two people in a double or twin room
♦◉	Dinner
Bft	Breakfast
K	Kitchen
NK	No kitchen
W	Washing Machine
D	Dryer
@	Internet access
X	Closed days or periods
CTR	Centro de Turismo Rural
①	Information centres/Oficinas de Turismo
⇨	Route finding guidance *always in bold italics*
⇨	General Advice in normal italics

1. Numbers

The figure immediately after a place name (pop) indicates the number of inhabitants. Altitude of places where known is given in metres. The other figure in **bold italics** on the right is the distance still to go in km to Santiago. As far as possible it refers to the route preferred by most pilgrims. It cannot be absolutely precise given the number of possible variations of the route.

The figures in brackets after an albergue indicate the number of bed spaces. Where known, the number of rooms is also given eg (35÷3). Most albergues now have a kitchen; though pans, plates and cutlery may not be provided. Almost all albergues have hot showers.

2. Times

All times are given in the 24-hour format.

3. Hotels and albergues

 In Spain, as elsewhere, hotel room rates vary with the season. Prices quoted are for one person (🚶) or two people sharing (🚶 🚶) unless otherwise stated. Other room options for three or more sharing may be available. **Check this and prices before booking.**

Opening times for *albergue*s will depend upon season, weather, etc. These are generally posted on their website or on the door of the albergue itself.

4. Church and Mass

Churches and times of Masses are given where they are known. The information is taken from www.misas.org & www.acogidacristianaenelcamino.es. Check locally for times of Masses as these often change in Summer and Winter. In smaller places listen for the church bell which often indicates Mass is about to start. Please email us with updated details of Mass locations and times.

5. Accommodation in winter

Many albergues close at the end of October until Spring. However this website maintained by Lourdes Lluch, hosptalera in Fromista lists the albergues which are open during winter: www.aprinca.com/alberguesinvierno

6. Maps and stages

The maps and elevation profiles provided in this guide are reproduced by the kind permission of www.gronze.com, a very useful online resource for pilgrims. Although the maps have to have a starting and end point we do **NOT** recommend these as set stages for walking the route. The ideal is to walk the distance with which you are comfortable and then use one of the many accommodation options.

Remember – You can help the pilgrims who come after you

The guides published by the Confraternity of Saint James are written by pilgrims who have walked the routes. They are kept up-to-date with information sent by other pilgrims who use the guides. Please help your fellow pilgrims by keeping notes and reporting any changes to the route or to the accommodation listed. **Please email office@csj.org.uk with any suggestions.**

Acknowledgements

We thank the following for their help in preparing this edition: www.gronze.com, Marcus Selle, Angelika Schneider.

¡Buen Camino!

River Nive & Clock Tower, Saint-Jean-Pied-de-Port

Saint-Jean-Pied-de-Port/Donibane Garazi (pop 1600 alt 163 m) 774

Saint-Jean-Pied-de-Port is a popular tourist destination, as well as being the departure point for many non-Spanish pilgrims. Hotel accommodation is relatively limited but there are many *chambres d'hôtes* (B&B) available in addition to the growing number of *auberges* (albergues) catering for the pilgrim trade. If you intend to stay in a hotel or a *chambre d'hôte* you should book well in advance. Saint-Jean has a wide range of shops, services and a tourist information centre.

Express Bourricot, based in Saint-Jean-Pied-de-Port, provides: a minibus service to Saint-Jean from a number of destinations, including Biarritz and Bilbao airports; a daily shuttle from Saint-Jean as far as Croix Thibault on the Route Napoléon; and to Roncesvalles on the road route for those who do not feel up to walking this first stage. Prices vary according to the numbers using the service as well as distance. ☎ 0661 960 476. www.expressbourricot.com

Camino Francés 2018/19

Church and Mass - *The 14th century red schist Gothic church, Notre-Dame-du-Bout-du-Pont, stands by the Porte d'Espagne (The Spanish Gate). The original was built by Sancho the Strong of Navarre to commemorate the 1212 Battle of Las Navas de Tolosa, where Moorish dominance of Spain was undermined.* **Mass 10.30am - but confirm time at church or Accueil Saint Jacques.**

A Call first at the *Accueil Saint Jacques (Pilgrims' Office)* at 39 rue de la Citadelle, which welcomes pilgrims and advises on the next day's journey over the Pyrenees to Roncesvalles. A *credencial* (or pilgrim passport) can be obtained for 2€. **Open all year**. Opening hours are 07.00-09.00, 11.00-12.30 and 15.30-21.30 although these may vary a little. It is staffed by pilgrims who speak a variety of languages; they will arrange albergue accommodation and provide information on weather.

Municipal Albergue (32÷3) 55 rue de la Citadelle - ♦ 10€ including bft. **K W D. Open all year.** ☎ 617 103 189. No advance booking.

Albergue Azkorria **PR** (8) 50 rue de la Citadelle - ♦ 29€. Meals. **W D @.** ☎ 559 370 053. www.hebergements-pays-basque.fr/accueil.

Albergue Beilari (18÷5) 40 rue de la Citadelle - ♦ 30€+ including ♦ & bft. **NK. X Oct-Mar.** Reservations can be made up to two weeks before arrival. ☎ 0559 372 468. www.beilari.info.

Albergue Compostella **PR** (14) 6 rue D'Arnegu - ♦ 12.5 – 15€. **K. Open all year.** ☎ 559 370 236.

Albergue Esponda (14) **PR** 9 rue du Trinquet - ♦ 14€. **K W @. Open all year.** ☎ 679 075 252. jeanmarie.mailharro@wanadoo.fr.

Albergue Kaserna **PR** 43 rue d'Espagne (12) - ♦ 15€ B&B. Meals. **W D.** ☎ 559 376 517 jacques.mullon@orange.fr.

Albergue Le Chemin vers l'étoile **PR** (20÷5) 21 rue d'Espagne - ♦ 17€ including bft. ♦ 10.50€. **W D. X Nov-Feb.** ☎ 0559 372 071.

Auberge du Pèlerin **PR** (48) 25 rue de la Citadelle - ♦ 17€. ♦ 15€ bft 5€. **W D. X Nov-Feb.** ☎ 0559 491 086. Email: contact@aubergedupelerin.com

Albergue Au Chant de Coq **PR** (8) 36 rue de la Citadelle - ♦ 15€. **X Oct-Mar.** ☎ 0674 310 283.

Albergue Zuharpeta **PR** 5 rue Zuharpeta (22) - ♦ 12.5€. Meals @. ☎ 559 373 588.

La Coquille Napolean (10) - ♦ 18€. ☎ 662 259 940 www.lacoquillenapoleon. simplesite.com.

H *Gîte Ultreia* **PR** (15÷4) 8 rue de la Citadelle - ♦ 16-17€. One twin room 44€ to 48€. bft 5€. **X Nov-Mar.** ☎ 0680 884 622. | *Le gîte du Camp Romain* (10), 4km before Saint-Jean at Saint-Jean-le-Vieux on the GR65 - ♦ 15€. ♦ ♦ 40-50€. **K W D.** ☎ 0686 998 203. | *Ramuntcho* 1 rue de France. Rooms from 66-98€. ☎ 0559 370 391. |

In Uhart-Cize, opposite the church is the useful *Hôtel Camou* - ♦ 45-55€.

Many hotels at all prices outside of the Old Town.

⇨ *Much of this stage of your journey is through the French part of the Basque country. Basque is one of the four official languages of Spain and many places have both a Basque and a Castilian/French name. Both names are given with the Castilian/French version first.*

⇨ ***There are two routes from Saint-Jean-Pied-de-Port to Roncesvalles/ Orreaga. a)*** *Route Napoléon.* ***This is harder, higher, and more spectacular but do not attempt it in bad weather. Less fit walkers, especially those on their first day, should leave early and be prepared for the route to take all day. Cyclists should be sure of their fitness. There is no problem using a bike, but some sections will need to be walked. b)*** *The Lower Route via Valcarlos* ***taken by most medieval pilgrims. This shadows what are today the D933 in France and the N135 in Spain. This is for less fit walkers and cyclists and it is the only feasible route in bad weather.***

Route Napoléon - 25 km by direct route, 26 km by Ibañeta variant.

THIS ROUTE IS CLOSED FROM 1 NOVEMBER TO 31 MARCH – USE THE LOWER LEVEL ROUTE VIA VALCARLOS DURING THIS PERIOD

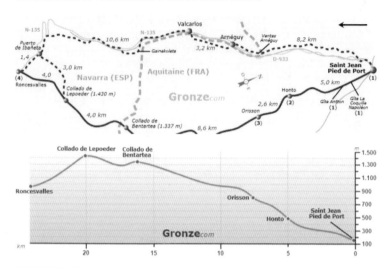

WARNING: This is a dangerous route in the months of short daylight hours and during these the police may close the route. Please observe the warning signs. Check local weather forecasts. Never start off later than 10.00. Buy provisions the day before. Water is scarce, so carry enough with you. In spring there may be melting snow on the route. You will see red and white flashes of the GR65 as well as the yellow arrows which you will follow all the way to Santiago.

⇨ **Apart from a short section after Honto the route follows the road (D428) for 15 km.**

5 km to Honto/Huntto (on D428 from Saint-Jean) (alt 520 m)   769

⇨ *This village is not signposted and is the last for 20 km*

H *Gîte d'etape - Ferme Ithurburia* (22) - 🛏 48€ including 🍽 & bft. Mme Ourtiague. **Open all year.** ☎ 0559 371 117.

A 3 km beyond Honto: *Albergue Kayola* **PR** (15) - ♦ 15€. **K.** ☎ 559 491 303 and *Albergue Refuge-Auberge Orisson* **PR** (18÷3) beds plus tents - ♦ 35€, including ⁜ & bft. **X Nov-Feb.** ☎ 0681 497 956. www.refuge_orisson.com.

Advanced reservations are recommended for these establishments.

⇨ *After Honto the road curves to the right while the waymarked path goes left. Cyclists should stay on the road, the waymarked path re-joins it later. Up to and beyond the Vierge de Biakotti, on the left, the route follows the road. Eventually you veer right off the road, well-marked with a memorial cross, onto a grassy track (not well-waymarked until after the cattle grid at the frontier).*

12 km to Col de Bentarte (1337 m), 16 km to Col de Lepoeder (1440 m), 20 km to Roncesvalles by direct route, 21 km by variant.

⇨ *Very well-waymarked in Spain. Fountain after the frontier. A long level stretch through beech woods then a climb to Col de Lepoeder. From here the roofs of the Abbey will be just visible far below. The direct route (4 km to the Abbey) is very steep. Cyclists, and in bad weather, take the variant to join the road route at Ibañeta 2 km away (then 3 km to the Abbey).*

On the Route Napoléon

Road or Lower Level Route Via Valcarlos

⇨ *The Accueil Saint Jacques tends to encourage pilgrims to take the Route Napoléon but the Lower Level Route is well-waymarked with a mix of yellow arrows, French GR route markings and new blue and yellow markers. Much of it is off road.*

Camino Francés 2018/19

8km to Arnéguy, the border between France and Spain (267 m)

⇨ *About 1 km out of Saint-Jean, the route leaves the D933 and turns right over a river, the Nive de Arnéguy, then follows a quiet country road to the Ventas: once duty-free shops. One has a bar and is open early. A good footpath brings you to Arnéguy itself, the border bridge and then via Ondarolle. This follows a quiet road, rejoining the main route at Valcarlos.*

H *Hotel Celementina* Rd 933 Le Bourg, 64220 Arnéguy, Francia ☎ +33 524 341 006. www.hotelclementenia.com

3 km to Valcarlos/Luzaide (alt 365 m)

A *Albergue Municipal Turístico* (24÷2) - ♦ 10€ including bft. Sheets & towels 3€. **W.** Advanced booking possible. ☎ 948 790 117 or 646 048 883. If closed ask at *Benta Ardandegia*, c/Elizaldea. **Open all year.**

H *Casa Marcelino.* ☎ 948 790 063. | *Casa Etxezuria.* ☎ 948 790 011. | *Hostal Maitena.* ☎ 948 790 210. All in c/Elizaldea. | *Apartamentos de Montaña Mendiola.* ☎ 609 755 105. www.turismomendiola.com.

Baker, shops and two banks. ⓘTourist information c/Elizaldea has internet connection.

☞ The church has a representation of Santiago Matamoros (St James the Moorslayer) and St James the Pilgrim. Ask for the key at *Bar Iñaki*. The owner will accompany you.

⇨ *Continue on the road until you see a sign close to km 61 indicating a turn downhill to the left to Ga*ñecolete, past *the hamlet following a small stream to re-join the main road. Stay on the road until you see another sign to the left. Follow this along a grassy path to reach Ibañeta.*

10 km (16 km by road) to Ibañeta (alt 1057 m) 749

☞ **Ibañeta marks the summit. A modern chapel has replaced the earlier chapel of Charlemagne. A sign in French, Spanish and Basque invites pilgrims to pray to Our Lady of Roncesvalles. Monument to Roland. This is where the variant of the *Route Napoléon* re-joins the *Camino*.**

3 km to Roncesvalles/Orreaga (pop 30 alt 960 m) 749

The Abbey is where the road route and the Route Napoléon merge. The monks of Roncesvalles have welcomed pilgrims since a hospital was founded here early in the 12th c. The collegiate church of the monastery, consecrated in 1219, is a fine example of French Gothic. Museum is free to pilgrims over 65 with *credenciales*. Reduced rate for others. It contains religious paintings and sculpture. Open in the summer Sat, Sun and festivals 11.00-13.30 and 16.00-18.00. The 14th c. royal pantheon, the former Chapter House, contains the 13th c. tombs of Sancho the Strong and his wife Doña Clemencia of Toulouse. As well as the church and cloister, see also the *Capilla de Santiago* (13th c. usually locked) and the 12th c, or earlier, *Capilla Sancti Spiritus*, also known as the *Silo de Charlemagne,* where monks and villagers are still buried. Roncesvalles is full of echoes of the *Song of Roland,* the great medieval poem recalling the events of August 778 when Charlemagne's rearguard was ambushed and Roland blew his horn to summon the Emperor. An ornate pilgrim cross, on the left when leaving the village, is a replica of a lost 14th c. original. Tourist Information Centre. **NOTE: At the bar book and pay before Mass for both restaurants.**

Church and Mass - Mass followed by a blessing for pilgrims 20.00 Mon-Fri, 18.00 Sat, 19.00 Sun.

Accommodation: for information on all accommodation available in Roncesvalles see: http://www.roncesvalles.es.

A *Albergue de la Colegiata Real*-Oficina del Peregrino (183÷4, 16 in low season) - ⫚ 12€. Priority for walking pilgrims. **W D**. Open 16.00-22.00. Leave 08.00. **Open all year.** http://www.alberguederoncesvalles.com.

H Co-located within the Abbey Estate, an attractive conversion into: *Casa de Beneficiados* consisting of apartments of various sizes and *Hotel Roncesvalles* with 16 well appointed hotel rooms. See www.hotelroncesvalles.com for more information. Prices start at 55€ for a single hotel room in the low season rising to 135€ for an apartment for four persons in high season. | *Casa Sabina* - ⫚ 44-55€. ⦿ 13-17€. Bft 3.50€. ☎ 948 760 012. Very popular. | *La Posada* - ⫚ 44-55€. ⦿ 10€. Bft 6.60€. **X Jan-Feb.** ☎ 948 760 225.

3 km to Burguete/Auritz (alt 892 m) 746

H *Hostal Burguete* - favoured retreat of Ernest Hemingway - ♦ 25-40€. ♦ ♦ 50-56€. Good bike storage. ☎ 948 760 005. www.hotelburguete.com. | *Hostal Jaundeaburre* c/San Nicolas 28 - ♦ ♦ 28€. **X Sept-Jul.** ☎ 948 760 078. | *Hotel Loizu* c/San Nicolas 13 - ♦ 53-63€. ⏹ 10€. ☎ 948 760 008. www.loizu.com. | *Don Jáuregui de Burguete* c/San Nicolás 32 - ♦ ♦ 50-56€. ☎ 948 760 031. www.donjauregui.com. | *Casa Rural Txiki Polit* av/Roncesvalles 42. ☎ 607 815 587. www.txikipolit.es. | *Casa Rural Pedroarena* c/Berexi 6. ☎ 948 760 164, 619 444 207. www.casapedroarena.com | *Casa Rural Bergara* c/San Nicolás 44. ☎ 948 760 044, 618 032 232.

Bank (with ATM), supermarket and pharmacy. Asador Ariza at entrance to village serves breakfast from 07.00.

4 km to Espinal/Aurizberri 742

3 bars, 2 restaurants, shop, baker, doctor.

A *Hostal Albergue Haizea* **PR** (28) - ♦ 12€. **X 2 weeks Nov**. ☎ 948 760 379.

Albergue Irugoienea **PR** (21÷2) - ♦ 11€. ⏹ 10.50€. Bft 3.50€. ☎ 649 412 487. www.irugoienea.com

14

H Casa-rural *Errebesena-Ohian-Eder* c/San Bartolomé 25. ☎ 948 760 141. www.casaerrebesena.com. Errebesena is a B&B with 8 double rooms - � 30€. � 40€. Ohain-Eder is for longer stays. | *Casa Rural Roncesvalles* c/San Bartolome, 86. ☎ 628 271 155. www.apartamentosirati.com. � 50€. �9090 60€. � 100€. | *Apartamentos Irate* San Bartolomé 80. ☎ 628 271 155. www.apartamentosirati.com. 4 apartments to be shared by up to 4 people and 1 for 2 people. Check the website for prices. | *Apartamentos Goizeder* c/San Bartolomé 3. ☎ 639 543 631. www.casagoizeder.com. 4 apartments 3 for 4 people and 1 for 5 people. Check the website for prices.

Campsites: 1.5km from the Camino - *Camping Urrobi* Class 2 site. **X Oct-Mar.** Has a small *albergue* - �9012€. Evening meal available.

The Pyrenees near Burguete

4.5 km to Viskarret/Biskarreta 738

H *Casa Rural Posada Nueva* **PR** c/San Pedro 28. � 35€. **Dec-Mar.** ☎ 948 760 173. www.laposadanueva.net. | *Pension El-La* c/San Pedro 19. ☎677 641 236. � 38€. | *Casa Rural Maitetxu* c/San Pedro, 12. ☎669 755 563, 948 760 175. www.casamaitetxu.com. | *Casa Rural Batit* c/San Pedro 18. ☎ 616 068 347. � 20€. | *Casa Rural Amatxi Elsa* c/San Pedro 14. ☎ 948 760 391, 626 166 538. � 35€. � 50€.

Camino Francés 2018/19

Bar Juan opens 8.00 - coffee meals & sandwiches. Shop on left leaving the village. *Sello* at church. **Sunday Mass 11.00.**

10.5 km to Esteribar/Zubiri (pop 459 alt 526 m) 727

A *Albergue Municipal* Old School House, avda/Zubiri (70÷2) - ♦ 8€. **X Nov-Apr.** Opens 12.00. ☎ 628 324 186.

Albergue Zaldiko **PR** (24÷3), just past the bridge on R - ♦ 10€. Owner will wash and dry clothes 6€. **NK,** but microwave and coffee machine. Free **@.** www. alberguezaldiko.com. Advanced booking advised. **X Dec-Feb.** ☎ 609 736 420.

Albergue El Palo de Avellano **PR** av/Roncesvalles 16 (57÷3) in 5 dormitories sleeping 8-12 people - ♦ 16€, including bft. ☺ 13€. Also two dbl. rooms and a family suite for 4 with en suite, 35-82€. **NK. X Dec-Apr.** ☎ 948 304 770. www. elpalodeavellano.

Albergue Río Arga Ibaia **PR** c/Puenta de la Rabia 7 (12) -⓪15€ B&B. **W D K @. Open all year.** ☎ 948 304 243. hrioarga@gmail.com.

Albergue Suseia **PR** c/Murelu 12 (22) - ♦ 15€ B&B. **K W D @. Open all year.** ☎ 948 304 353. www.suseiazubiri.com.

Albergue Segunda Etapa **PR** av/de Roncesvalles, 22 (12÷2) - ♦ 13€. **K @.** ☎ 697 186 560, 948 304 170. info@alberguesegundaetapa.com. www. alberguesegundaetapa.com

H *Pensión Zubiaren-Extea,* located just before the bridge into town, on your left - ♦ 30€. ♦ 48€. ☎ 948 304 293. Mb +34 618 014 515. NB Arrive before 5pm. Washer €3.50, but no dryer. | *Pension Goikoa* av /Roncesvalles 12 - ♦ 18€. Private rooms with shared bathroom. | *Hosteria Zubiri.* At southern end of the village, 10 rooms - ♦ 52-60€ B&B. ☺ 19€. ☎ 948 304 329. | *Hostal Gau Txori,* on main road at northern end of village - ♦ 38€. ☺ 13-20€. **X Dec-Jan.** ☎ 948 304 076. | *Bar Pensión Amets* c/Gerestegui 25. 4 rooms plus kitchen - ♦ 30-35€. **X Nov-Feb.** ☎ 948 304 308. | *Usoa* Puente de la Rabia 4 - ♦ ♦ 25-35€. ☎ 948 304 306. | *Zubiaren Etxea* c/Camino 2 - ♦ ♦ 25-35€. ☎ 948 304 293.

Polideportivo in sports centre has 11€ *Menú.* Shop next to the church.

Church and Mass - *Church of San Esteban, Plaza de la Iglesia.* **Evening Mass.** Confirm at church or listen for bells.

☞ Zubiri (the name means "the bridge village" in the Basque language, Euskera) is the main city in the area. The medieval bridge, the Puente de la Rabia, which crosses the Rio Arg,a is the subject of local legends, including the belief that the bridge had healing powers and that the relics of Santa Quiteria are buried in one of the pillars of the bridge. Adjacent to the bridge once stood the pilgrim hospital of Santa Magdalena. In the 19th century there were a series of civil wars in Spain called the Carlist Wars. During one of these the the church was used as a barracks and was destroyed in 1836.

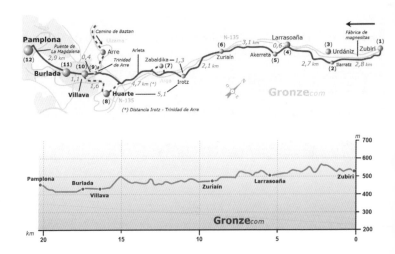

⇨ *After Zubiri the* camino passes through the Magna Mining complex and up to the hamlet of Ilarratz. Approximately 100 metres further down the road from Ilarratz, on the right hand side of the road, is the the Abbey of Eskirotz and Ilarratz. The buldings originate in the 12th century and incorporate the former parish church of Santa Lucia. Having been in ruins for many years the site has been purchased by two pilgrims who wish to restore the Abbey as a resting place for pilgrims. Visitors are welcome. See: https://www.facebook.com/theabbey.es

2 kms beyond Zubiri in Itlarratz *Albergue Ezpeleku* **PR** c/San Martín 3 (6÷1 + 1 double) - ▐ 15€. ▐ ▐ 48€. **K W D @. Bkfast 4.50€.** ☎ 948 304 721, 696 808 894, 609 415 741. albergueezpeleku@gmail.com. www.albergueezpeleku.com

3kms beyond Zubiri in Urbániz *Albergue Acá y Allá Urdániz* **PR** c/San Miguel 18 (6) - ▐ 18€ B&B. Meals. **K W D @.** ☎ 615 257 666. www.alojamientosacayalla. com/urdaniz.

5.5 km to Larrasoaña/Larrasoaina 722

A *Municipal Albergue* (56÷4) - ▐ 8€ + 1€ for bedding. Microwave. **@.** Small shop selling tinned food. **X 10 Dec to 10 Jan.**

Albergue Bide Ederra **PR** c/San Nicolas 27 (4) - ▐ 15€ B&B. **K W D @.** ☎ 948 304 692. www.hostelbideederra.com.

Albergue San Nicolas **PR** c/Sorandi 5-7 (40) - ▐ 12€. **K W D @.** ☎ 619 559 225. www.alberguesannicolas.com.

H *Pensión El Peregrino* (4) - ▐ 32€. **W. Open all year.** ☎ 948 304 554. | *Pensión El Camino/Café Larrasoaina* c/Portalcelay 12 (3 rooms) - ▐ ▐ 50€. ▐ 15€. Bft 4€. **X Oct-Mar.** ☎ 948 304 250. | *Pensión Tau* c/Errotabidea 18. ▐ ▐ 50-60€, also triples and a quadruple. ☎622 745 620, 607 849 540. www.pensiontau. com. | *Pensión Casa Elita* c/Amairu 7. ▐ ▐ 60€. ☎948 304 449, 609 756 891. www.casaelita.es

Bridge over Río Arga

1 km to Akeretta

H Hotel Akerreta c/Transfiguración 11 - ♦ 57€. ⦿ 19€. **X Jan-Feb.** ☎ 948 304 572

In the next stretch of approximately 6kms there are two albergues approx 3 kms apart:

A *Zuriáin La Parada de Zuriáin* c/Landa 8 (16) - ♦ 12€. **X Nov-Feb.** ☎ 699 556 741

A *Zabaldika* (18) - ♦ donativo. **X Mid Oct-Mid April.** ☎ 948 330 918.

11.5 km to Arre 711

On the outskirts of Villava, a town with all facilities.

A *Trinidad de Arre monastery* (34÷3) - ♦ 8€. On the right on far side of Villava Bridge. Opens 12.00. **W.** Lounge and Garden. **Open all year.** ☎ 948 332 941.

Church and Mass - *Comunidad Marista de Trinidad.* **Mass 19.30 with pilgrims' blessing.**

Albergue Municipal Villava c/Pedro de Atarrabia 17-19 (54) - ♦ 9€. **W D K @.** ☎ 948 331 971. www.alberguedevillava.com.

H *Hotel Villava* avda/Pamplona - ♦ 45€. ⦿ 13€. ☎ 948 333 676. | *Pensión Arkano Etxea* Grupo Martiket 6 - ♦ 25€ B&B. ⦿ possible. ☎ 696 597 140.

Huarte/Uharte is between Arre and Pamplona, but a few kilometres off the camino. About 500m beyond Arre, a road to the left, signed for Huarte, will take you there.

A *Municipal Albergue* (60÷5) pl/San Juan 1 - ♦ 10€. In a large well equipped building. Pilgrims can stay more than one night. Consistently good reports. **X Dec-Mar.**

4.5 km to Pamplona/Iruña. (pop 191000 alt 415 m) 707

The first major city on the route. Head for the Plaza del Castillo, the centre for much of the activity in the city.

ⓘ Avda Roncesvalles 4. Mon-Fri 10.00-14.00 & 16.00-19.00. Sat 10.00-14.00. ☎ 948 206 540.

Pamplona has been the capital of Navarra since the 9th c. and before that it was a powerful fortress town defending the northern approaches to Spain over the Pyrenees. Founded by the Romans as Pompaelo in 75 AD.

The *Catedral de Santa María* is situated in the Old Town or the *Casco Viejo* and is built on the same site as the ancient Roman city of **Pompaelo. The Cathedral** is an excellent example of the architecture of the Gothic period of the 14th and 15th centuries and is home to the largest number of important relics and works of art in the city. For 300 years the Cathedral was the seat of the Royal Court and was the scene of coronations and meetings of parliament. The neoclassical façade was designed by by Ventura Rodríguez. It contrasts with the **Gothic** interior where in the 28-metre-high central nave lies the **tomb of Carlos III of Navarre and his wife, Eleanor of Castile.** However the greatest feature of this Cathedral is its **cloister**, considered among the most impressive in the Gothic world. Of particular note: The gothic style cloister with 24 pointed arches and five doors. The wood and silver carving of Santa María la Real from the 12th century and the Barbazana chapel.

The Diocesan Museum (10.00-13.30 & 16.00-19.00, Sun 10.00-14.00) 3.60€, is housed in the old refectory and kitchen and entered via the cloisters.

Behind the Cathedral is one of the oldest parts of the city and the best preserved parts of the city walls. Museo de Navarra (Tues-Sat 10.00-14.00 & 17.00-19.00, Sun 11.00-14.00) 2€. Archeology, history of Navarre and an art collection, including a Goya portrait. The 13th c. church next to the museum has a statue of St James over the main altar.

Church and Mass - *The Cathedral of Santa María la Real.* **Mass at 10.30, Sunday 10.00 and 12.00.**

Warning: *It is very difficult to find any accommodation in Pamplona during the annual festival of* ***San Fermín (July 6 to 14)*** *the world famous 'running of the bulls'.*

A *Albergue Iruñako Aterpea* **PR** c/Carmen 18 (24) - 🚹 15€ B&B. **@.** ☎ 685 735 595. www.alberguedepamplona.com

Albergue Plaza Catedral **PR** c/Navarrería 35 (46) - 🚹 🚹 15-18€ B&B. **K W D @. Open all year.** ☎620 913 968.

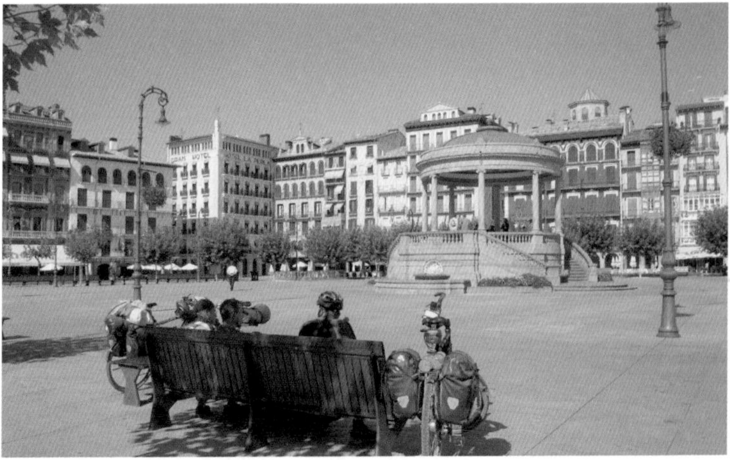

Plaza Mayor, Pamplona

Albergue Aloha **PR** c/Sangüesa 2, 1st floor (22) - 🚹 15€ B&B. **K W D @. Open all year.** ☎ 648 289 403. www.alohahostel.es

Albergue Ibarrola **PR** c/Carmen 31 (20) - 🚹 18€ B&B. **W D @. Open all year.** ☎ 692 208 463. www.casaibarrola.com

Albergue Paderborn Playa de Caparroso 6 (26) - 🚹 6€. **B W D @.** ☎ 948 211 712. www.jakobusfreunde-paderborn.eu

Albergue Ciudadela **PR** c/Ciudadela 7 (24) - 🚹 16€. **W D K @. Open all year.** ☎ 948 983 884.

Municipal Albergue De Jésus y María c/Compañía 4 (112) - 🚹 8€. **W D @.** ☎ 948 222 644.

Albergue Hemingway **PR** c/Amaya 26 (30) - 🚹 🚹 15-18€. **W D K @. Open all year.** ☎ 948 983 884

Albergue Xarma **PR** Av. Baja Navarra 23 (22) - 🚹 15€+ B&B. **K W D @. Open all year.** ☎ 948 046 449. www.xarmahostel.com

Casa Ibarrola c/del Carmen 31 (20) - 🚹 18€. **Open all year.** ☎ 692 208 463. www.casaibarrola.com

Albergue Juvenil Fuerte del Principe c/Goroabe 36. International YHA. Membership needed. (16, in dorms) - 🚹 5€, 29 yrs & under, 11€ over 30 yrs. Rooms also available. **@**. Meals (14.00-22.00). **X Oct-June.**

H There is a wide variety of hostel and hotel accommodation available in Pamplona. Here are some suggestions received from pilgrims: *Pensión Arrieta,* c/Arrieta, central. ☎ 949 228 459/652 849 209 www.pensionarrieta.net. | *Pensión Escaray,* c/Nueva central - 🚹 20€. 🚹 🚹 40€. ☎ **948 227 825.** www.pensionescaraypamplona.com. | *Hostal Bearán* c/San Nicolas 25. In the Old Town a few minutes walk from the Plaza del Castillo - Singles 35€. Doubles 45€. ☎ **948 223 428.** www.bearanpamplona.com. | *Alojamientos Iruña* avda/ Pio XII. 32 rooms and apartmement for up to 6 people - 🚹 🚹 45€. Rooms with balcony. ☎ 948 277 780. www.alojamientosiruna.com.

See also https://www.gronze.com/etapa/zubiri/pamplona.

⇨ ***Camino route through Pamplona: Portal de Francia, calles Carmen, Navarreria, Mercadores, Plaza Ayuntamiento, San Saturnino, Mayor, el Bosquecillo, Navas de Toloso, Pio XII, Vuelta del Castillo and Fuente de Hierro.***

The waymarking on the way out of Pamplona to the south takes you either across or around a large park. Some bars open at 06.30.

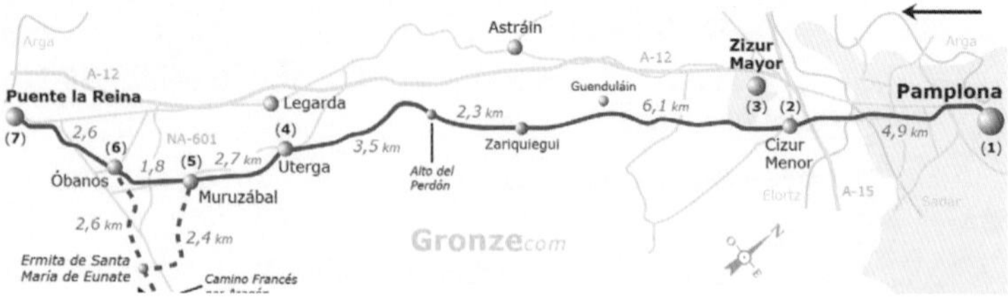

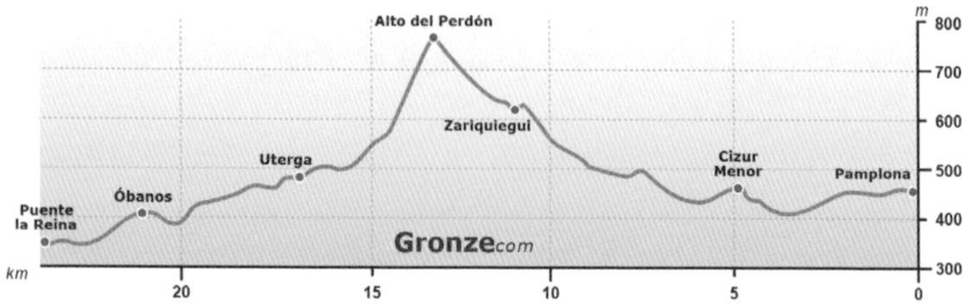

4.5 km to Cizur Menor/Cizur Txiki 702

Church and Mass - *Iglesia de la Encomienda de la Ordén.* **Sunday Mass at 18.30.**

A *El Albergue Privado Familia Roncal* **PR** (52) - ♀ 12€. **W.** Nice garden. **X** Nov. ☎ 948 183 885. In the centre of the village. Popular. www.elalberguedemaribel.com

Albergue Encomienda de San Juan (27) - ♀ 7€. **X Nov-Mar.** ☎ 616 651 330. **K.** Run by the Knights of St John of Malta. On left at entrance to the village. Opens 12.00. Overflow housed in medieval church nearby.

H *Rte. Asador el Tremendo* has a pilgrim menu and is popular with pilgrims. Bar behind *farmacia* also does meals. Shops and several bars. Cycle shop, *Cyclos Cizur* ☎ 948 172 282.

⇨ *The route from Cizur to Puente de la Reina crosses a mountain ridge (Alto de Perdón) with a line of wind turbines and silhouettes of pilgrims. The descent has recently been improved, but is still not easy for cyclists.*

Alto del Perdón

6 km to Zariquiegui 696

A *Albergue San Andrés* **PR** (18÷2) in 2 rooms - ♦ 8€. ⦿ 10€. Bft 2€. ☎ 948 353 876. Open 09.00-22.00. Bar and food available all day. www. alberguezariquiegui.com. | Shop - *La Tienda Mertxe,* open 10.30-14.00.

6 km to Uterga 690

Albergue-Rte Camino del Perdón **PR** (16÷1) c/Mayor 57 - ♦ 10€. ⦿ 12€. Plus 4 dbl rooms - ♦ ♦ 50-65€. **X Oct-Mar.** ☎ 948 344 598. www.caminodelperdon.es

A *Casa Baztán* **PR** c/Mayor 46 (24) - ♦ 10€. ♦ ♦ 45€. **X Nov-March.** ☎ 948 344 528. www.alberguecasabaztan.com

1.5 km to Muruzábel 687

Small village with 2 albergues and a hostal. Bar Los Nogales has a menú.

A *Mendizabel* c/Mayor 7 (10) - ♦ 18€. ☎ 948 344 169. May lend a cycle to visit Eunate.

A *El Jardín de Muruzábel* c/Monteviejo 21 (26) - ♦ 10€. ♦ ♦ 40 €. ☎ 696 688 399. www.alberguejardindemuruzabal.com

H *Casa Villazón* c/Rebote 5 - ♦ 25€. ♦ ♦ 35€. ☎ 620 441 467. www. casavillazon.com

⇨ **If making the detour to the Church of Saint Mary of Eunate, turn left past the church. NB There is no longer an albergue at Eunate.**

The Church of Saint Mary of Eunate lies on the Monreal/Las Campanas road, 3 km off the Camino. The 12th c. octagonal church is surrounded by a series of arches. Opinions vary as to its origins. It may have been a Knights Templar church or it may simply have been a pilgrims' burial ground. Recommended. Check opening times.

⇨ *If not taking the detour to Eunate, turn right just after the village.*

2 km to Obanos 685

A *Albergue Usda* **PR** c/San Lorenzo (36÷3). Bunks in rooms of 6-20 persons - 8€. Bft 3€. Open 13.30- 22.00. **X Nov-Mar. ☎** 676 560 927.

Albergue Atseden **PR** Camino de Santiago 2 - ♦ 12 €. ☎ 646 924 912. atseden1234@gmail.com. www.atsedenhostel.com

H *Hostal Mamerto* Obanas, small hotel - ♦ 30€. ♦ ♦ 45€. ☎ 649 139 611, 948 344 344. www.hostalmamerto.com. | *Apartamentos Rurales La Patxuela* - Obanas on the Camino - sleeping up to 17 people in 2 apartments. Telephone or check website for availability and prices. ☎ 639 320 025, 620 281 381. www.lapatxuela.com | *Casa Rural Raichu* c/Larrotagaña 2. ♦ 30€. ♦ ♦ 45€. ♦ ♦ ♦ 80€. ☎ 948 344 285, 686 679 415, 600 202 917. www.casaraichu.com. | *Casa Rural Villazón II* trav/San Sebastián 5. ♦ ♦ 45€. ☎ 620 441 467, 948 277 391. www.casavillazon.com

Rte. Ibarberoa, c/San Salvador (behind the church) ⭐ 9.50-10.50€. Open for lunch, closed evenings, except Fri/Sat in summer. Two bars, shop and a health centre.

Between Obanos and Puente la Reina, the two pilgrim routes over the Pyrenees, one from Roncesvalles and the other over the Somport Pass (the route from Arles) meet. A modern (1965) statue of a pilgrim marks the spot.

Puente La Reina

2.5 km to Puente la Reina/Gares (pop 2,155 alt 346 m) 683

The attractive town of Puente la Reina owes its name to Queen Doña Mayor, wife of Sancho Garcés III, el Mayor (King of Navarre 1005-1035). She ordered the construction of the beautiful bridge over the river Arga to make the route for pilgrims to Santiago easier. The bridge, with six arches and five pillars, is one of the most beautiful structures on the route. The church of Santiago has a notable statue of Saint James inside. *Iglesia del Crucifijo* (church of the Crucifixion) originally founded by the Knights Templar in the 12th c. The porch is decorated with scallop shells. At one side is the original pilgrims' hospice, one of the oldest still extant.

Church and Mass - *Iglesia de Santiago.* **Daily 10.00 (Sunday 12.00) and 19.30.**

ⓘ Casa del Vínculo, c/Mayor 105.

A *Padres Reparadores* c/Crucifijo 1 (100÷10) - ♦ 5€. Small **K @ D.** Space to camp behind the albergue. **Open all year. 12.00-20.00.** ☎ 948 340 050. www.economo.puente@esic.es

Albergue Santiago Apóstol **PR**, 300 m uphill after the Puente de Peregrinos (100÷5) - ♦ 10€. **NK.** Bar. ♦❙ 10€. Bft 3.50€. **W D @.** Open 12.00-23.00. ☎ 948 340 220. www.alberguesantiagoapostol.com

Albergue Hotel-Albergue Jakue **PR** c/Irunbidea (36÷2) - 10€. ♦❙ 13-23€. **W D @.** Bike storage. **X Nov-Mar.** Open 12.00-22.00. Hotel accommodation - ♦ 45-50€. ♦❙ 13-23€. **Open all year.** ☎ 948 341 017. www.jakue.com

Albergue Estrella Guía **PR** Paseo de los Fueros 34 - 2º Piso (6) - ♦ 12€ B&B. **M W D @. Open all year.** ☎ 622 262 431.

H *Hotel Rural El Cerco* c/Don Rodrigo Ximenez de Rada 36 - ♦ 45-50€. Bft 5€. Bike storage. ☎ 948 341 269. | *Hotel Bidean* c/Mayor 20. Has 20 ensuite rooms plus restaurant - ♦ 40€. ♦ ♦ 57€. **NB** Arrival before 4pm. ☎ 948 341 156. www.bidean.com | *Hotel Ganbara* c/Mayor 86 - ♦ 25€. ♦ ♦ 40€. ☎ 948 341 186. http://www.artesaniaganbara.com

Bar la Torreta has 9.50€ *menu*. Opens at 06.30 in summer.

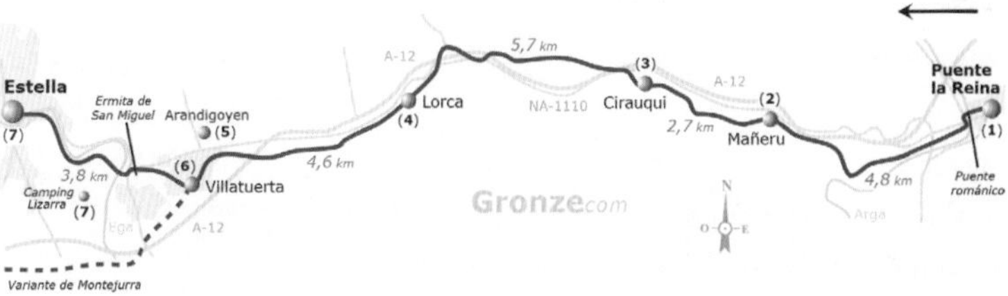

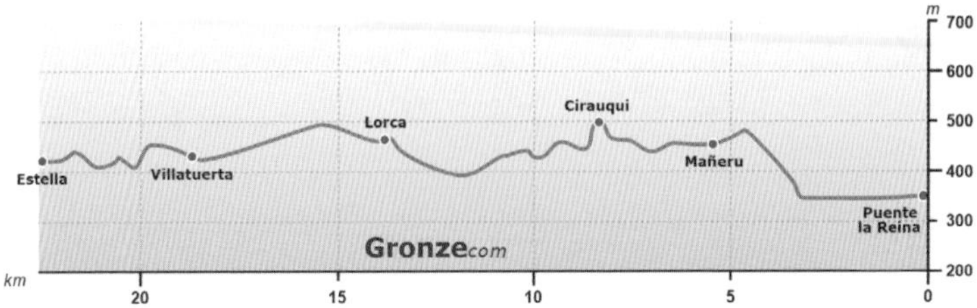

4.5 km to Mañeru 678

2 bars, 2 food shops and *farmacia*, all near the church.

A *El Cantero* c/Esperanza 2 (26) - 👤 11€. **X Nov-April.** ☎ 948 342 142. www.albergueelcantero.com.

H *Casa Rural Isabel* c/Caridad 5 - 👤 👤 40€. ☎ 948 340 283.

3 km to Cirauqui (pop 500 alt 505m) 675

A *Albergue Maralotx* **PR** (28÷3) c/San Roman 30 - 👤 11€. **NK.** 🍽 11€. **W D.** Coffee machine. Two dbl rooms with bath - 42€. **X Nov-Feb.** ☎ 678 635 208.

Food shop and panadería, both open by 08.30. Four bars.

☞Ancient restored hilltop village. Churches of San Roman, 12th & 16th c, and Santa Catalina, 13th c. Fine stretch of Roman road and bridge. *Río Salado*, between Cirauqui and Lorca is mentioned in the 12th c Pilgrim Guide - Book 5 of the manuscript compilation known as the *Liber Sancti Jacobi* or *Codex Calixtinus*. The water was reputed to be bad and horses that drank it did not survive. This was known to the local population who would not tell pilgrims but would wait with knives so that they could skin the dead animals.

5 km to Lorca 670

A *Albergue de Lorca* **PR** c/Mayor 40 (13) - ♦ 7€. Free @. **X Nov-Mar.** ☎ 948 541 190. www.alberguedelorca.com

Albergue La Bodega del Camino **PR** (30÷4) - ♦ 8-10€. ♦ ♦ 20-40€. ▣ 10€. **W D. X Nov-Easter.** ☎ 948 541 162. www.labodegadelcamino.com

H *Casa Rural Txema* c/Mayor 17 - ♦ ♦ 70€. ♦ ♦ ♦ 90€. ☎ 676 554 744.

Bodega Molina serves a 6€ *menú* from 13.00. *Bar-Tienda Izcue*, on way out of the village, open from 07.00. Panadería in the church square is open from 05.30.

The Church of Santa Maria 12th & 16th c. has a recently restored *retablo*.

5 km to Villatuerta 665

A *Albergue Privado La Casa Mágica* **PR** (40÷5), in rooms of five to ten persons - ♦ 14€. ▣ 13€ (vegetarian). Bft. **W D @. X Nov-Feb.** ☎ 948 536 095.

The Church of the Asunción, which you can see from afar, has 15th c. frescoes and altarpiece and a Romanesque door. If locked try 8 Plaza Iglesia; Sra Elisa has a key and a *sello*.

4 km to Estella/Lizarra (pop 13000 alt 426 m) 661

A beautiful town that has always been associated with the pilgrimage. Rich in monuments and has a charter dating back to 1090. The city is dominated by the fortified pilgrimage church of San Pedro de la Rúa notable for its great tower, Romanesque interior and the beautiful Romanesque cloister, with two wings (the other two were destroyed in 1572). The church dating from the 12th century is the oldest in the city. The pórtico, with a series of lobed arches shows clear Moorish influences. The church has three naves that house various artistic treasures, among which are the sculptures of San Andrés and San Pedro, a Romanesque Virgin, a Gothic statue of Our Lady of the O, the Romanesque stalls of the choir and a baptismal font. The cloister is impressive particularly the beautifully sculpted capitals.

Visits to the interior are 19.30-20.00. Ask at the ⓘ c/San Nicolás 1. Mar-Dec, Mon-Fri 10.00-14.00 & 16.00-19.00, Sat-Sun 10.00-14.00. ☎ 948 554 011. The *turismo* has a *sello*. Next to the *turismo* is the *Palacio de los Reyes de Navarra,* (the palace of the Kings of Navarre), 12th c. - a rare example of large-scale Romanesque civil architecture. Part is now an art gallery devoted to the painter Gustave de Maetzu.

Estella

Church and Mass - *Iglesia de San Miguel, Plaza de San Miguel,* has a north doorway that is one of the gems of the Camino. ***Mass: Wed, Fri and Sat 19.00, Sun 11.30, with pilgrim blessing.***

A *Albergue Municipal* (96÷5) c/de la Rúa 50 - ⵏ 6€, sheets included. **W D. X Dec-Jan.** ☎ 948 550 200. Open 11.30-22.00 HS, 1400-22.00 LS. Leave 08.00.

Albergue Parochial San Miguel (30÷2) c/Mercado Viejo 18 - *Donativo,* including evening meal and bft. Open 12.00-22.00.

Albergue Anfas (34÷1) c/Cordeleros 7 Bajo - ⵏ 7€. **K W D. X Oct-Mar.** ☎ 948 554 551. Open 13.00-22.00. Run by a charitable organisation supporting people with learning difficulties. www.albergueanfas.org

Albergue Capuchinos Rocamador c/Rocamador 6 (54) - 👤 13€. **K W D @. Open all year.** ☎ 948 550 549.

Youth Hostel Oncineda c/Monasterio de Irache 11 (95) - 👤 10€. **K W D.** ☎ 948 555 022. www.albergueestella.com.

Albergue la Hostería de Curtidores **PR** c/Curtidores 43 (30÷5) - 👤 15€. 👤 👤 45€. **K W D @.** ☎ 948 550 070, 663 613 642. curtidores@albergueestella.com. www.lahosteriadelcamino.com.

H *Hostal Cristina*, c/Baja Navarra 1, 1st floor (13 rooms) - 👤 38€. 👤 👤 45€. ☎ 948 550 450. | *Hostal El Volante*, travesia Merkantondona 2 - 👤 30-45€. 👤 👤 52-62€. ☎ 957 553 948, 638 029 005. www.hostalelvolante.com. | *Hotel Yerri,* av. Yerri 35 (28 rooms) - 👤 48€. 👤 👤 70€. ☎ 948 546 034. www.hotelyerri.es

Estella has many other small reasonably priced hotels and restaurants.

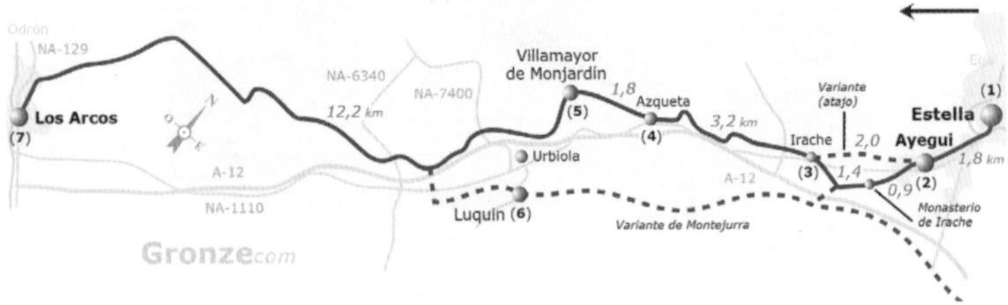

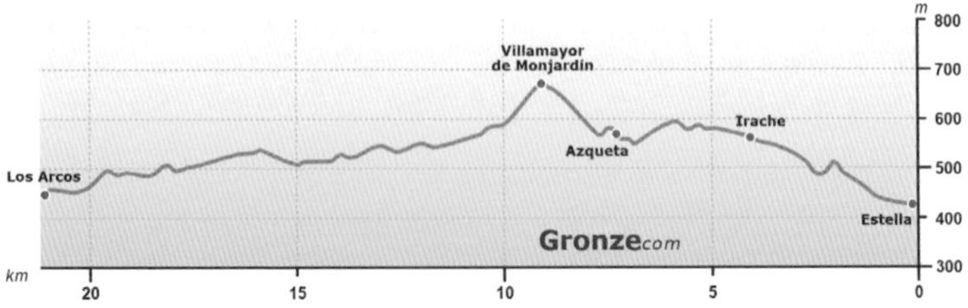

2 km to Ayegui 659

A *Albergue Municipal San Cipriano* (60÷3) - 10€. 9€. Bft 4€ (served from 05.30). **W D** @. Bike storage. **Open all year.** ☎ 948 544 311. Large supermarket nearby. Those who stay here can obtain an *Ayeguina*, a certificate for having completed the first 100 km from Saint-Jean-Pied-de-Port.

H. Bars, restaurants and shops.

0.5 km to Monasterio de Irache 658

☞ Just before the 12th c. Cistercian monastery and Church of Irache, is the *Fuente del Vino* (the Wine Fountain) provided by the winery. It starts running at about 08.30. The monastery has been restored and is open Mon-Fri 09.00-13.30 plus Wed-Fri 17.00-21.00. Sat-Sun 09.00-13.30 & 16.00-18.00. Pleasant picnic area nearby,

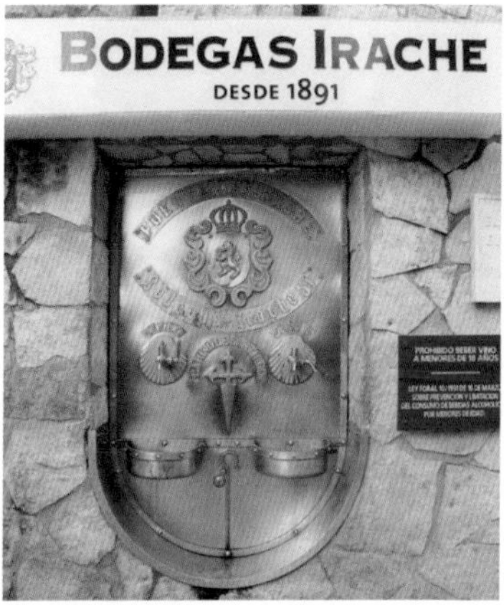

Wine Fountain, Irache

H *Hotel Lurgorri* Prado de Irache 7 - 40€. 55€. Bft included. in *Cafetería-Bar Urbasa* 11€. Swimming pool & laundry. ☎ 948 558 286.

Camping Iratxe av/Prado de Irache 14. Accommodation in rooms and bungalows. 28€ +. Bunglalow 42€+. ☎ 948 558 286. www.campingiratxe.com

5 km to Azqueta 654

Albergue Hosp. La Perla Negra **PR** (7) c/Carrera - ♦ 25€ B&B + evening meal. **M W @**. ☎ 627 114 797.

Bar and *fuente*.

2 km to Villamayor de Monjardín 652

A *Albergue Hogar Monjardín* (25÷5) at c/Plaza - ♦ 8€. ▮● 10€. Bft 5€. **X Nov-Mar.** ☎ 948 537 136. Run by OASIS, a Dutch group.

Albergue Villamayor de Monjardín **PR** (20÷3) - ♦ 15€, bft & sheets included. 1 dbl - ♦ ♦ 45€. **X Nov-Mar.** ☎ 948 537139.

H *Casa Rural Montedeio* c/Mayor 17 - ♦ 35€. ♦ ♦ 45€. ☎ 676 187 473. www.casaruralmontedeio.com

Bar-restaurante *Ilarria* offers a 10€ Pilgrim *menú*.

On the way to Los Arcos

12 km to Los Arcos (pop 1,418 alt 450m) 640

Church and Mass - *The Iglesia de Santa María* 12th c to 18th c. has gothic cloisters. ***Mass at 19.30 daily and Sun at 12.30. Pilgrims' blessing.***

The church of Santa María de los Arcos is one of the most outstanding churches in Navarra. It is a building of considerable presence with rich decoration in its design. The church was built and then renovated in a number of stages during the twelfth, thirteenth, sixteenth, seventeenth and eighteenth centuries. Therefore several styles are evident from the Romanesque, Gothic, Renaissance and Baroque periods. Often in the church new decorative features were laid upon previous structures. The great Baroque altarpiece is a central feature of the church with rich carving surrounding the figure of Our Lady. Other notable altar pieces in the church are those in the altars of Saint John the Baptist, the Virgin of the Rosary, Saint Francis Xavier and in the chapel of Saint Gregorio Ostiense.

The church has a single nave and boasts three other very significant features – the carved stonework in the choir executed in the late Renaissance Mannerist style, the striking 18th century organ held to be one of the finest instruments of its type in Navarra and the late 16th century cloister.

A *Albergue Casa de la Abuela* **PR** (24) pl/de la Fruta 8 - ♦ 10€. Bft 3.50€. 4 dbl rooms 35-45€. **K W D.** Open 12.00. **X Nov-Feb.** ☎ 948 640 250. www.casadelaabuela.com

Albergue Municipal Isaac Santiago (70) c/San Lázaro - ♦ 6€. **K.** Open 12.00-22.00. Depart 08.00. **X Nov-Mar.** ☎ 948 640 230. www.campus-stellae.org. Run by Flemish Friends of St James. On way out of town behind school.

Albergue La Fuente-Casa de Austria **PR** (47÷3) c/travesía del Estanco 5 - ♦ 9€. 5 dbl rooms - ♦ ♦ 35€. Bft 3€. **K W D.** Open 12.00. **X Dec-Jan.** ☎ 948 640 797

Albergue Casa Alberdi **PR** (26) c/Hortal 3 - ♦ 10€. Plus 2 rooms - ♦ ♦ 40€. **K W D.** Open all year. 13.00-23.00. ☎ 948 640 764

H *Hostal Ezequiel* La Serna 14 (12 rooms) - ♦ 25-42€. ♦ ♦ 55-59€. Bft 7€. ☎ 948 640 296. | *Hotel Monaco*, Plaza del Coso 1 - ♦ 39-49€. ♦ ♦ 50-69€. English speaking owner. ☎ 948 640 000. | *Pensión Mavi* c/Medio 7 - ♦ ♦ 50€. ☎ 948 640 081. www.pensionmavi.es | *Pensión Ostadar* c/San Lázaro 9 - ♦ 35€. ♦ ♦ 50€. ☎ 649 961 440. www.pensionostadar.com | *Hostal Suetxe* c/Carramendavia - ♦ 49€. ♦ ♦ 55€. ☎ 618 724 437. www.hostalsuetxe.es

Several small bars, restaurants and shops. Health centre ☎ 948 640 800.

ⓘ Plaza de Cozo.

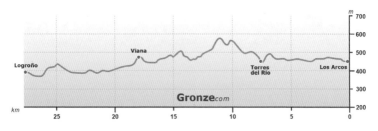

6 km to Sansol 633

A *Albergue Arkadi y Nines* **PR** (14÷2) c/Taconera, 10 rooms sleeping 4-8 people - 🚹 6€. **K.** Open 13.00-23.00. Depart 10.00. **X Nov-Palm Sunday.** ☎ 680 679 065

Albergue Deshojando **PR** (24) c/Barrio Nuevo 4 - 🚹 10€. **M W D @.** ☎ 948 648 473

Albergue Codés **PR** (24÷2) c/Los Bodegones - 🚹 12-15€. **M W D @.** ☎689 804 028. alberguerestaurantecodes@gmail.com www.alberguerestaurantecodes.com

H *Casa Rural El Olivo* c/Taconera 9 - 🚹 25-35€. 🚹 🚹 40-45€. Including bft. 🍴 10€. **Open all year.** ☎ 948 648 345.

Bar de Socios - sandwiches and hot dishes 07.30-23.00 in summer, 10.00-15.00, 16.30-22.30 in winter. Health centre and *farmacia* in village.

1 km to Torres del Rio 632

NB The spring just before the village near the bridge is *non potable* ('not drinkable').

A *Albergue Mariela* **PR** (50÷5) pza/Padre Valeriano Ordoñez 6 - ♀ 10€. Bunk beds in 5 rooms. **@.** Bft 3.50€. **Open all year.** ☎ 948 648 251. At top of hill entering the village.

Albergue Pata de Oca **PR** (44) c/Mayor 5 - ♀ 10€. Bft 3-6€. ♦ 10€. **Open all year.** ☎ 948 378 457. www.lapatadeoca.com

H *Hotel San Andrés* c/Jesús Ordoñez 6, pool and restaurant - ♀ 40€. ♀ 60€. ♀ ♀ 75€. ☎ 948 648 472. www.sanandreshostal.com.

2 bars - *El Mesón* has *sello*. ATM, two small supermarkets and a medical centre.

☞ Octagonal Romanesque Church of Santo Sepulcro. Clear *mudéjar* influence. Well worth a visit. Check outside church for keyholder or ask at *El Mesón*. Church is open during the day with volunteer attendants. (1€ donation suggested).

11 km to Viana (pop 3,276 alt 466 m) 621

Church and Mass - *Iglesia de Santa Maria (13-17th c. Gothic) Cesare Borgia died in the village and his remains are buried in the church, which has an outstanding Renaissance Porch.* **Mass daily at 19.30 (Sun 11.00) with pilgrim blessing.**

A *Alberguería Andrés Muñoz* (46÷4) - ♀ 8€. **K @.** Bike storage. **Open all year.** 12.00-22.00. ☎ 948 645 530. Located end of town, near the ruined Church of San Pedro.

Parochial Albergue of Santa María (16÷4), mattresses on the floor - *Donativo*. An evening meal may be served and bft. Opens 17.00. **X Oct-May.**

Albergue Izar **PR** (22÷1) c/El Cristo 6 - ♀ 8-10€. ♀ ♀ in dbl room 30€. Bft 3€. **K.** Open 12.00-22.00. **X Nov-Feb.** ☎ 948 090 002. www.albergueizar.com.

H *Hotel Palacio Pujadas*, c/Navarro Villoslado 30 - ♀ 50€. ♀ ♀ 70€. Bft 2.90€. ☎ 948 646 464. The bar opens by 08.00. **Closed for Christmas holiday.** | *Casa Armandariz* c/Navarro Villoslado 19 - ♀ 24€. ☎ 948 645 078. www. sidreriacasaarmendariz.es. | *Pension San Pedro* c/Medio San Pedro 13 - ♀ 30€. ♀ ♀ 40€. ☎ 948 645 927. www.pensionsanpedro.com.

Just before Logroño, you leave Navarra to enter the wine producing region of La Rioja.

Santa María La Redonda

9 km to Logroño (pop 128,000 alt 384 m) 612

☞ A large Cathedral city which is the capital of La Rioja. The heart of the city is the Paseo del Espolón. ⓘ c/Portales 50. The previous Collegiate church was given the designation Cathedral by Pope John 23 in 1959. Parts of the interior are from the 15th century with the façade being added in the 18th century. The Cathedral has the figure of St. James carved in the choir stalls. In the Plaza San Agustín is the *Museo de la Rioja*, which contains many religious objects rescued from abandoned monasteries in the area. Tues-Sat 10.00-14.00 & 16.00-21.00, Sun 11.30-14.00. Free.

Church and Mass - *Near the iron bridge over the river is the Gothic Church of Santiago el Real, 16th c. with a splendid statue of Santiago Matamoros over the main entrance.* **Mass 08.30 and 19.30 daily (Sun 10.30 & 19.30).**

A *Albergue Municipal* (64÷3) c/Rúavieja 32 - ♦ 7€. **K @.** Bike storage. **Open all year.** 12.30-22.00. ☎ 941 230 545. Near Church of Santa María del Palacio. Turn right at end of bridge into Rúa Vieja. The albergue is run by the local pilgrim association.

Albergue Parochial (30) c/Barriocepo 8 - Donativo. ▌●▐ and bft. In the parish hall of the Church of Santiago el Real (see note above). Facilities are limited, one toilet and shower for men and one for women. Bunks (limited) and mattresses on the floor. Open June-Sept only but from Oct-May 18 places are available at Barriocepo 58.

Hostel-Albergue Entresueños **PR** (100) c/Portales 12 - ♦ 10€. 5 rooms. ♦ ♦ 38-50€. **K. Open all year and all day.** ☎ 941 271 334.

Albergue Albas **PR** (22) Plaza Martínez Flamarique 4 bajo 1 - ♦ 12€. **W D. Open all year.** 11.00-22.00, but call in winter.

Albergue Check in Rioja **PR** (30) c/Los Baños 2 - ♦ 12€. **W D @.** ☎ 941 272 329.

Albergue Santiago Apóstol **PR** (78) r/Vieja 42 - ♦ 10€. **K W D @. Open all year.** ☎ 941 256 976.

Albergue Logroño **PR** (48) c/Capitán Gallarza 10 - ♦ 10€. **M W D @. Open all year.** ☎ 941 254 226. www.alberguelogrono.es

Residencia Jorbalande de la Religiosas Madres Adoratrices 8 c/Juan XXIII - ♦ 9€. Good facilities. **July-Aug only.** ☎ 941 259 974.

There is a good selection of hostel and hotel accommodation available in Logroño at all prices. These include:

H *Pensión Sebastián* ☎ 941 242 800 - ♦ 20€. ♦ ♦ 35€. ♦ ♦ ♦ 50€ - and *Pensión San Juan* - ♦ 30€. ♦ ♦ 50€. These are both at c/San Juan 21 (just north of the main square) www.pensionsebastian.com | *Hotel Isasa*, c/Los Doctores Castroviejo. Prices seasonal - ♦ 30-50€. ♦ ♦ 50-65€. ☎ 941 256 599. www.hotelisasa.com | *Pensión Berceo* c/Gonzalo de Berceo 8 - ♦ from 25€. ♦ ♦ from 40€. ☎ 619 655 593. www.pensionberceo.com | *Pensión Rey Pastor* c/Rey Pastor B&B - ♦ 25€. ♦ ♦ 45€. ☎ 941 206 552. | *Hotel Murrieta**** Calle Marqués de Murrieta, 1 - ♦ €54. ♦ ♦ 50-70€. ☎ 941 224 150. www.hotel-murrietalogrono.com. | *Camping La Playa* Av. de la Playa 6 - bungalows ♦ ♦ 50€. Tent 12€. ☎ 941 252 253. www.campinglaplaya.com

☞ **Detour to Clavijo 40 km.** The village of Clavijo, 18 km south of Logroño, is the site where legend has it that in 844 St James miraculously appeared on his white charger to help the Christians. The castle at Clavijo is in a spectacular setting with a cross of Santiago erected by the council of the Military Orders. On the hillside opposite is a hermitage of St. James. Enquire at Tourist Information in Logroño about buses to Clavijo and accommodation there.

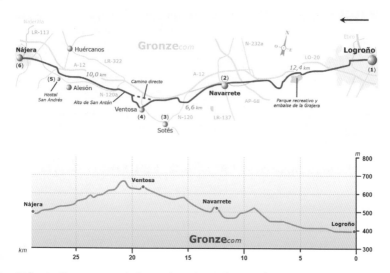

13 km to Navarrete excl. detour (pop 2000 alt 555 m) 599

⇨ *Walkers should take great care when joining the N120 before entering Navarrete, as traffic comes round a blind bend in both directions.*

Just before entering Navarrete the Camino passes the restored remains of the pilgrim hospital of St John of Acre. On the right of the camino in the centre of c/Mayor is the 16th c. Church of La Asunción

Church and Mass - *Iglesia de La Asunción de Nuestra Señora, Plaza Gonzalo Sáenz, 1.* **Mass daily 19.30, Sunday 9.30 and 13.00.**

A *Albergue Municipal* (46÷4) c/San Juan 2 - 🚶 7€. **K W D.** Leave by 08.00 **X Nov-Feb.** ☎ 941 440 722. Admission priorities: (1) walkers of more than 20 km (e.g. Viana); (2) walkers of less than 20 km (eg Logroño); (3) cyclists.

Albergue El Cantáro **PR** (22÷2) c/Herrerías 16 - 🚶 10€. Bft 3€. 🍽 10€. **K.** Lockers with keys bike storage. Also has rooms with bath at 35-40€. **Open all year.** 11.00-23.00. ☎ 941 441 180.

Albergue A la Sombra del Laurel **PR** (32) c/de Burgos 52 - 👤 15€. **W D @.** ☎ 639 861 110. www.alasombradellaurel.com

Albergue Buen Camino **PR** (10) c/La Cruz 2 - 👤 10€. **K W D @.** ☎ 941 440 318. www.alberguebuencamino.es

Albergue La Casa de Peregrino **PR** (14÷2) c/Las Huertas 3 - 👤 10€. Bft 2.50€. 🍽 5€. **K.** Also has 3 bedrooms - 👤 👤 25€. Open 11.00-23.00. **X Nov-Mar.** ☎ 630 982 928

Albergue Camino de las Estrellas (40) crta/Burgos 9 - 👤 10€. 👤 👤 40€. All year. Bike storage. ☎ 618 051 392. wwwalbergueelcaminodelasestrellas.com

H *Hostal Villa Navarette* c/La Cruz - single 30€, double 40€, triple 54€ and quadruple 64€. Bft 3€. ☎ 941 440 318, 681 252 222. www.hostalvilladenavarrete.com. | *Hotel El Rey Sancho***,* on the Camino in the heart of the village at c/Mayor 5 - 👤 50€. 👤 👤 70€ (check if pilgrim discount). Three star hotel with all facilities and smart restaurant. ☎ 941 441 378. www.hotelreysancho.es. | *Hostal La Carrioca* c/Prudencio Muñoz 1 (the main road at top of town) - ☎ 941 440 805. 🍽 7.50€. Bft 2.50€. *Kairo's Café* next door is the same business.

Rte El Molino 🍽 9€. *Bar Deportivo* 🍽 12€. *Bar Los Arcos,* next to Municipal albergue, serves simple meals and bocadillos and has a *sello.*

On leaving town look for a cemetery on the left. It has a 13th c. Romanesque portal, originally the door to the pilgrim hospital of Saint John. **Optional route via Sotes**

A *Albergue San Martin* **PR** (10) c/San Miguel 67 - 👤 10€. Bft 3€. 🍽 10€. **K. X Nov-Mar.** ☎ 941 441 768. alberguesotes@gmail.com

Albergue Bodega Fernando J. Rodriguez **PR** (18÷1) c/Conde de Garay 25 - 👤 15€. **X Nov-Apr.** ☎ 670 053 229. alberguesotes@yahoo.es

Direct route 7 km to Ventosa 592

A *Albergue San Saturnino* **PR** (42÷6) c/Mayor - 👤 10€. **K W D.** Good reports. **Open all year.** 13.00-22.00. ☎ 941 441 899

H *Casona de las Aguedas* - 👤 55-65€. 👤 👤 65-70€. 🍽 20€. **Open all year.** ☎ 941 441 774. www.hotellasaguedas.com

Vineyards of La Rioja

9 km to Nájera (pop 6901 alt 485 m) 583

A *Municipal Albergue* (90÷1) Plaza de Santiago - *Donativo*. Good facilities. **K W** 3€. **D** 2€. Open 13.00 or 15.00-22.00. Leave 07.30. **Open all year.**

Albergue Puerta de Nájera **PR** (30) c/Ribera del Najerilla 1 - ♦ 10-15€. Two rooms - ♦ ♦ 30-40€. Open 11.00-23.00. **X Dec-Feb. ☎** 941 362 317.

Bar & *Albergue La Judería-Sancho III* **PR** (10) c Constantino Garrán, 13 - ♦ 10€. Bft 3.50€. ⑩ 9€. Four rooms - ♦ ♦ 30€. **Open all year.** 12.00-22.00. **☎** 941 361 138

Albergue Calle Mayor **PR** (17) c/Cicarán 5 - ♦ 9€. **M @. ☎** 941 360 407. www.alberguecallemayor.com

Albergue Nido de Cigueña **PR** (20) c/Cuarta San Miguel 4 - ♦ 10€. ♦ ♦ 15€. **W D V @. ☎** 941 896 027. www.alberguenajera.es

H *Pensión Calle Mayor* c/Cicarán 5 - ♦ ♦ 30€. Open 12.00-22.00. **X Nov-Mar. ☎** 941 360 407. | *Hostal Cuidad de Nájera* (8) - ♦ 20€. Eight rooms at ♦ 44-49.50€ and ♦ ♦ 51-60€. **X Christmas & New Year.** | *Hostal Hispano*, c/La Cepa 2, very easy to find from bus station – away from bridge. ♦ 35-38€. ♦ ♦ 50-52€. Bft 7-10€. **☎** 941 363 615. www.hostalhispanonajera.com. | *Hotel Duques de Nájera* c/Carmen 7 - ♦ ♦ 50€. **☎** 941 410 421. www.hotelduquesdenajera.com

Mesón La Amistad 🍽 7€. Café by bus station opens for bft on Sundays. Café/bar *Los Parrales*, pilgrim meal €12 - very good. ⓘ Plaza San Miguel, 10. ☎ 941 360 041

Río Najerilla, Nájera

The town is dominated by the 15th/16th c. monastery of Santa María la Real, originally a Cluniac foundation. The church contains the tomb of Blanche of Navarra, many other royal tombs and a Renaissance cloister. Closed Mondays. The large municipal swimming pool complex across the river is free to pilgrims with a ticket from the albergue.

☞ **Detour to San Millán de la Cogolla.** A variant of the route, well waymarked with yellow arrows and direction change signs, follows the *Camino Medieval* and the *Camino Real* for 16 km from the albergue at Nájera to San Millán and the two monasteries of Suso and Yuso. Suso is the upper Visigothic monastery, dating from the 11th c, the monumental Yuso down in the valley is mainly 16th to 18th c. The tomb of San Millán has a life size effigy of him surrounded by pilgrims. A guided tour is the only way to see Yuso. Both are closed on Mondays, except in August. Follow the Lr 206 from San Millán to rejoin the Camino at Azofra, about 13 km.

H Part of the Yuso monastery has been converted into a 4 star hotel - 🛏 72€. ☎ 941 373 277. There are also other accommodation options listed on www.booking.com

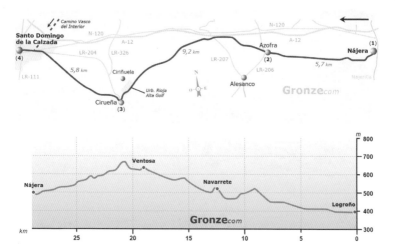

5.5 km to Azofra 577

Church and Mass - *Iglesia de Nuestra Señora de los Angles 17th and 18th c.* **Mass Wed and Fri 19.45, Sat 18.45, Sun 11.45. Check winter times at the church.**

A Municipal & Parish *albergues Herbert Simon* (60÷30) c/Las Parras - ♦ 7-15€. **K W D**5€ **@**. Open 12.00-22.00. **X Nov-Mar.** ☎ 941 379 220. The old parish albergue is used when the new albergue is full (26÷2).

H *Pensión La Plaza* Plaza de España 7 - ♦ 30€. ♦ ♦ 45€. ☎ 629 828 702. www.pension-la-plaza-azofra.com.

Three bars, two do bft 2€. *Bar Sevilla* near *La Fuente* has rooms 12€ and a good *menú* at 9€. Opens 18.00. Also 2 small shops and a *panadería*.

9 km to Cirueña 568

A *Albergue La Virgin de Guadalupe* **PR** (30÷5) Barrio Alto 1 - ♦ 7-10€. ♦ 7€. Bft 3€. **NK.** ☎ 638 924 069. Open 13.30-22.00. **X Nov-Mar.**

Albergue Victoria **PR** (8) prado/San Andrés 10 - ♦ 20€. ♦ ♦ 40€. ♦ 8-10€. Bft 3-5€. **Open all year.** ☎ 941 426 105. albergue@casavictoriarural.com

The fields out of Cirueña

H *Casa rural Victoria* (12) Pza/del Horno 8 (5 rooms) - ♀ ♀ 40€. ⦿ 8-10€. Bft 3-5€. ☎ 941 426 105. www.casavictoriarural.com

6 km to Santo Domingo de la Calzada (pop 5308, alt 639 m) 562

ⓘ Casa de Cultura c/Mayor 70. Jul/Sep, Mon-Sat 10.00-14.00 and 16.30-19.30. Sun 10.00-14.00.

Santo Domingo, after whom the town is named, was a Benedictine monk who devoted his life to pilgrims in the 11th c. He tended the sick, building a hospital, and paved roads and a bridge - hence his name (*calzada*=causeway) - and finally, in 1044, founding the town itself. The causeway survives at the end of town on the road to Burgos. He is buried in the Cathedral. The Cathedral, begun in 1158, was one of the earliest Gothic constructions in Spain, although it was not completed until the 16th c. There is a dominant detached Baroque tower.

Baroque Tower of Santo Domingo de la Calzada

The Legend of the Hen and Rooster Miracle
– from the Cathedral of Santo Domingo

"Legend tells of a German Pilgrim called Hugonell who was walking to Santiago with his parents, when they decided to rest at an inn in Santo Domingo de la Calzada. The owner of the inn´s daughter immediately fell in love with him; however her feelings were not reciprocated, so the girl, angered, placed a silver cup into his luggage and accused the boy of theft. Thieves at that time were punished by hanging, and this was the fate of Hugonell. His parents, saddened by his death, continued the pilgrimage, and upon arriving in Santiago de Compostela, began their return journey to visit the grave of their dead son. When they arrived in Santo Domingo however, they found their son still hanging in the gallows but, miraculously, alive. Hugonell, excited, said to them: "Santo Domingo brought me back to life, please go to the Mayor´s house and ask him to take me down". Quickly, the parents arrived at the Mayor´s house and told him of the miracle.

44

The incredulous Mayor, who was preparing to have dinner with friends, responded: "That boy is as alive as these two roast chickens we are about to eat," and, suddenly, the chickens came to life, sprouted feathers and beaks and began to crow... and so, to this day there is a saying about the town which goes: "Santo Domingo of the Way, where the roosters crow after being roasted".

In front of the Mausoleum there is a stone, polychrome and gothic Henhouse, which was built in the middle of the 15th century to keep alive a hen and a rooster in memory of the most famous of Santo Domingo´s miracles. There are documents from Pope Clemente VI dated 1350 allowing these live animals inside the Cathedral. Below the cage is a representation of the pilgrim being hanged painted by Alonso Gallego. Above the cage there is a piece of wood from the gallows".

Church and Mass – *Catedral.* **Mass daily at 20.00, followed by pilgrim blessing.**

A *Albergue Casa de la Confradía del Santo* (220÷10) c/Mayor 42 - ╫ 7-10€. **K.** Cyclists welcome but priority to walkers. **Open all year.** Opens 12.00-23.00 (summer), 12.00-22.00 (winter). *Credenciales* available. Pleasant garden where the spare cocks and hens for the Cathedral are housed. Coin operated launderette opposite the albergue.

A&H *Abadía Cisterciense de la Asúncion albergue* (40÷5) c/Mayor 29 - ╫ 6€. **K.** Open 12.00-22.00. Leave by 08.00. **X Oct-Apr.** ☎ 941 340 700. The Cistercian nuns also welcome pilgrims at the *Hospedería Cisterciense.* The entry to the Hospedería is c/Pinar 2 - ╫ 39-50€. ╫ ╫ 58€. ▮❶. Bft 4-7€. Doors locked at 23.00.

H *Hostal* San *Miguel* Paseo De Los Molinos 2, 1º - ╫ from 20€. ╫ ╫ €42. ☎ 600 212 691. www.pensionmiguel.com. | *El Corregidor* c/Mayor 14 - ╫ 40€. ╫ ╫ 60€. ☎ 941 342 128. www.hotelelcorregidor.com. | *Rey Pedro I* c/San Roque 9 - ╫ 40€. ╫ ╫ 50€. ☎ 941 341 160. www.hostalpedroprimero. es. | *El Molino de Floren* c/Margubete 5 - ╫ ╫ 59€. ☎ 941 342 931. www. elmolinodefloren.com. | *Parador de Santo Domingo de la Calzada* Plaza del Santo 3, former pilgrim hospice, historic building - ╫ ╫ 90€. ☎ 941 340 300. www.paradores-spain.com. | *Parador Bernardo de Fresneda* Plaza de San Francisco 1 - ╫ ╫ 75€. ☎ 941 341 150. www.paradores-spain.com

Plus several other *hostales* and *pensiones.* At a more economic level, *Bar Albert* Plaza Harmosilla 6 has rooms - ╫ 18€. ▮❶ 9€. ☎ 941 340 82.

A *Albergue Municipal Nuestra Señora de Carrasquedo* (42) - ╫ 8€. **M W D @. Open all year.** ☎ 627 341 907. Ermita 45, 1km before Grañon, www.carrasquedo.obr.es

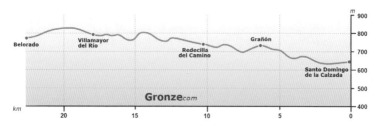

6 km to Grañón (pop 600 alt 724 m) 556

Church and Mass - *Iglesia de San Juan Bautista constructed 15th & 16th c.* **Mass daily 19.00, Sun 13.00 (not July and August). Evening prayer for pilgrims.**

A *Parochial albergue San Juan Bautista* (40÷2) in the bell tower of the parish church - *Donativo*. **Open all year.** Bikes accepted.

Albergue Ave de Paso **PR** (10) c/El Caño 18 - ♦ 10€. **M K W @.** ☎ 666 801 051.

Albergue Casa de Las Sonrisas **PR** (20) c/Mayor 16 - Donativo, no reservations. **Meals. @. Open all year.** ☎ 687 877 891.

H *Casa Cerro de Mirabel* c/Mayor 40 - ♦ ♦ 50€. ☎ 941 420 798. www. casacerrodemirabel.es. | *Casa Jacobeo* c/Mayor 34 - ♦ ♦ 50€. ☎ 941 420 684.

Plus 3 bars, 2 shops, 3 *panaderías, farmacia,* bank. Shop facing the church opens early.

Soon after Grañón, you leave La Rioja and enter the autonomous region of Castile and León, Province of Burgos.

Passiflora (passion flowers)

4 km to Redecilla del Camino 552

A *Albergue Municipal Hospital de San Lázaro* (36÷4) c/Mayor 24 (opposite the church) - ✝ 5€. **W.** Bar. Swimming pool in summer. **Open all day, all year.** ☎ 947 588 078.

Albergue Essentia (10) c/Mayor 34 - ✝ 10€. **Open all year.** ☎ 606 046 298.

H *Hotel Redecilla del Camino* c/Mayor 12 - ✝ 40€. ✝ ✝ 60€. ☎ 947 585 256. www.hotelredecilladelcamino.com

☞ A small village with a church with a Romanesque font.

2 km to Castildelgado 550

A *Albergue Bideluze* (16) c/Mayor 8 - ✝ 10€. **Open All Year.** ☎ 616 647 115. www.alberguebideluze.com.

H. Modern roadside hotel *El Chocolatero,* 37 bedrooms - ✝ 22-25€. ✝ ✝ 40-50€. ▮◉▮ 12.50€. Bft 5€. **Open all year.** ☎ 947 588 063. www.elchocolatero.es

Camino Francés 2018/19

⇨ Waymarked route takes you off the main road briefly forking left to Viloria de la Rioja. Signposted *'cuna de Santo Domingo'* (ie his birthplace), rejoining the main road 2 km later. There is an alternative route from Redecilla to Belorado, 1 km longer and away from the main road, but it is not waymarked.

1 km to Viloria de la Rioja 549

A *Albergue Acacio y Orietta* **PR** (10÷1) c/Nueva 6 - ♦ 6€. ᵀᴼᴵ & bft donativo. **@. Open all year.** ☎ 947 585 220. www.peregrinando.org.

Albergue Parada Viloria **PR** (16) c/Bajera 37 - ♦ 5€. **Meals. K W D @.** ☎ **639 451 660.**

H *Hotel Mihotelito* pl/Mayor 16 - ♦ ♦ 72€. ☎ 947 585 225, 676 390 240. www.mihotelito.es

3 km to Villamayor del Rio 546

A *Albergue San Luís de Francia* **PR** (26÷9) ctra/Quintanilla - ♦ 5€. Bft 3€. ᵀᴼᴵ 8€. Sandwiches. **W D.** Open 13.30. **X Nov-Feb.**

H *Casa Rural La Aldea Encantada* - ♦ 39€. ♦ ♦ 50€. ᵀᴼᴵ 15€. Bft 3.50-7€. **Open all year.** ☎ 947 580 484. Take RH turn just before Villamayor to Quintanilla del Monte. www.laaldeaencantada.es

5 km to Belorado (pop 2000 alt 760 m) 541

Church and Mass - *Iglesia de Santa María la Mayor - Late Gothic 16th c with chapel of Santiago.* **Mass May - October 19.00. Sunday 12.30.**

A *Albergue Parochial* (24) c/El Corro, next to the Church of *Santa María,* in an old theatre - *Donativo.* **X Dec-Apr.** Doors locked 22.00. ☎ 947 580 085.

Albergue Cuatro Cantones (62÷5) c/Hipolíto López Bernai - ♦ 7-11€. ᵀᴼᴵ 11€. Bft 4€. **K W D.** Pool. Open 11.00 (14.00 in winter)-22.00. **X Nov-Feb.** ☎ 947 580 591.

Albergue Caminante (22) c/Mayor 36 - ♦ 6€. ᵀᴼᴵ 10€. Bft 3€. Also has 8 rooms - ♦ 20€. ♦ ♦ 35-45€. **W D.** Open 10.00-22.00. **X Nov-Feb.** ☎ 947 580 231.

Municipal Albergue El Corro (40) c/Mayor 68 - ♦ 7€. **W D K @. Open all year.** ☎ 947 580 683. www.alberguemunicipalelcorro.es

Albergue El Salto (24) c/Los Cauces - ♦ 15€. Bike repairs. ☎ 669 415 639. www.elsalto.eu

Altar in Santa María Church

A&H *Hostal-Restaurant-Bar-Albergue A Santiago* Camino de Redoña (88÷8) - ☥ 5€. **NK. W D.** Pool**.** Albergue **X Nov-Mar**. Also Hostal with 12 bedrooms - ☥ 30€. ☥ ☥ 40€. **Open all year.** ☎ 947 562 164.

Hostel Puntob (13÷1) c/Cuatro Cantones 4 - ☥ 12€, plus rooms. ☥ 35€. ☥ ☥ 45€. ☎ 699 538 565, 947 581 620. hola@hostelpuntob.com www.hostelpuntob.com

H *Pensión Toni* Calle Redecilla, 7 - 1ºB (next to the Post Office) - Rooms: singles 31€, twin 47€. Triple and quadruple available. ☎ 947 580 525, 616 010 808 www.pensiontoni.com. | *Casa Rural Verdeancho* c/El Corro 11 (on way into town) - ☥ 36-42€. Serves Bft. ☎ 947 580 261. www.casaverdeancho.com. | *Casa Waslala* c/Mayor 57 - ☥ 25€. ☥ ☥ 42€, including ⊓⊙⊢ & bft. ☎ 947 580 726, 647 102 254. www.casawaslala.com

Camino Francés 2018/19

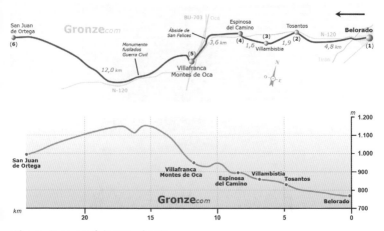

5 km to Tosantos (alt 818 m) 536

A *Albergue San Francisco de Asis* (30÷3) c/Santa Marina - *Donativo*. Mattresses on the ground (no beds). Meal and bft. Open all day. **X Nov-Feb.** Prayers after supper.

Albergue Los Arancones **PR** (16) c/de la Iglesia - ⍊ 10€. **W D @.** ☎ 693 299 063.

☞ 16th c Chapel of Virgen de la Peña. Key from house opposite, No 18. One bar on main road.

2 km to Villambistia 534

A *Albergue Municipal San Roque-Bar* (14÷1) - ⍊ 6€. ⍾ 9.50€. **W D. X Weds & Christmas/New Year**. Possibility of camping in the summer. www.villambistia.es

H *Hotel Rural Casa de los Deseos* c/Las Eras 16. ⍊ 25€. ⍊ ⍊ 35€. ☎947 108 588, 653 326 020. www.casadelosdeseos.es

1.5 km to Espinosa del Camino

A *Albergue la Campana* **PR** (10÷2) - ⍊ 17€ inc ⍾ and bft donativo. **X Dec-Jan**. ☎ 678 479 361. Priority to pilgrims on foot carrying their own pack.

Albergue Espinoso del Camino **PR** (10) c/Barruelo 2 - ⍊ 5€. **W D. Open all year.** ☎ 630 104 922.

A small friendly bar on the camino sells a selection of food and canned drinks.

5 km to Villafranca Montes de Oca (pop 230 alt 948 m) 526

A *Albergue Municipal* (60÷4) c/Mayor 17 - ♀ 5€. **K. Open all year**, and all day until 22.00 or 22.30. ☎ 947 582 149.

Albergue San Antón Abad **PR** (41÷2) - ♀ 5-10€. ⫯⫯ 12-15€. Bft 4-8€. **K.** Also a hotel with 14 rooms - ♀ 60€. ♀ ♀ 70€. *Albergue* **X Dec-Feb.** ☎ 947 582 150. The hotel website *www.hotelsanantonabad.*com has a section on the albergue.

H *Hostal El Pájaro*, Carretera principal - ♀ 20€. ♀ ♀ 36€. Bft (from 07.00) 4€. ⫯⫯ 10€. Bike storage. ☎ 947 582 029. | Casa Rural Alpargateria c/Mayor 2, B&B - ♀ 20€. ♀ ♀ 36€. ☎ 636 751 656. www.casaruralalpargateria.es. | *Pensión Jomer* c/Mayor 52 - ♀ ♀ 55€. ☎ 947 582 146.

Basic shop in Bar *El Puerto and* ☞ Church of *Santiago*

Take care here. The road through the village is very busy with many fast moving heavy vehicles.

The next stretch of the camino consists largely of a waymarked forest path that passes a monument to a group of local people executed during the Spanish Civil War. Cyclists can take the road route to Valdefuentes, a 7 km climb to the col de la Pedraja. There is the gothic chapel of Santiago (locked) in a rural setting by the Rio Roblegardo.

Forests after Villafranca Montes de Oca

Camino Francés 2018/19

12 km to San Juan de Ortega (pop 20 alt 950 m) 517

San Juan de Ortega was a disciple of *Santo Domingo de la Calzada* who worked with him on the building of bridges in the area. The large Romanesque pilgrim Church of San Nicolás and monastery have been restored, and a crypt built for the Saint's tomb. A tiny hamlet. Not on all maps but clearly signposted down quiet roads.

Church and Mass - *Iglesia de San Juan de Ortega (Barrio San Cristobal).* **Mass 18.00 (not December - March).**

A *Monasterio de San Juan de Ortega (70÷3)* - ♦ 7€. **X Nov-Feb.** ☎ 947 560 438. Wardens in summer. Family and group rooms. www.alberguesanjuandeortega.es

H *Hostal Rural La Henera*, 10 rooms - ♦ 40€. ♦ ♦ 50€. Bft 3-4€. **X Nov-Feb.** ☎ 606 198 734. **Warning** - must arrive before 3pm. www.sanjuandeortega.com.

Bar Taberna Marcela next to the monastery - some meals. Open for breakfast at 08.00. Summer only. No shop.

⇨ **Shortly after San Juan de Ortega, there is a large noticeboard giving details of an alternative route to Burgos, via several villages.**

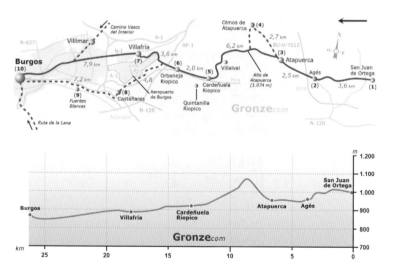

3.5 km to Agés 513.5

A *Albergue Municipal Taberna de Agés* (36÷1) c/de Medio 19b - 🚹 8-12€. 🍽 9-11€. Bft 2-4€. Sandwiches. Cycle repairs. Open 11.00-23.00. Leave 06.00-09.00. **X Jan.** ☎ 947 400 697.

Albergue El Pajar & la Casa Roja **PR** (68) c/Paralela del Medio. In 2 houses. El Pajar (34÷4) - 🚹 9-10€. Casa Roja (30) - 🚹 5€. 🍽 10€. Bft 3€. **W D.** Cycle repairs. Open all day. **X Nov-Feb.** ☎ 947 430 388.

Shop and cafetería *El Alquimista,* calle Ochabro 2.

2.5 km to Atapuerca 511

Albergue El Peregrino (36÷10) ctra/105 - 🚹 8€. **K W D.** Cycle repairs. 6 rooms - 🚹 or 🚹 🚹 35€. Open 13.00-22.00, depart 08.00. **X Nov-1 Mar.** ☎ 947 580 882.

A&H *Hostal Rural Papasol & La Hutte* (18) La Hutte is run as an albergue - 🚹 5€. 🍽 12-15€. Bft 3€. The Hostal has 7 bedrooms - 🚹 38-44€. 🚹 🚹 50-68€. **Open all year.** ☎ 947 430 320. | **H** Pensión Restaurante *Bar El Palomar* c/la Revilla 22. 4 rooms - 🚹 🚹 40€, bft included. 🍽 10-13€. ☎ 947 400 675. | *Casa Rural El Pesebre* c/Iglesia 16. 🚹 45€. 🚹 🚹 55€. ☎ 610 564 147, 645 109 032. www.elpesebredeatapuerca.es

Restaurante *Comosapiens* Camino de Santiago 🍽 12-20€.

☞ Village with an important archaeological site.

⇨ **At the end of the village the camino turns left uphill. To get to Olmas and its albergue continue on this road.**

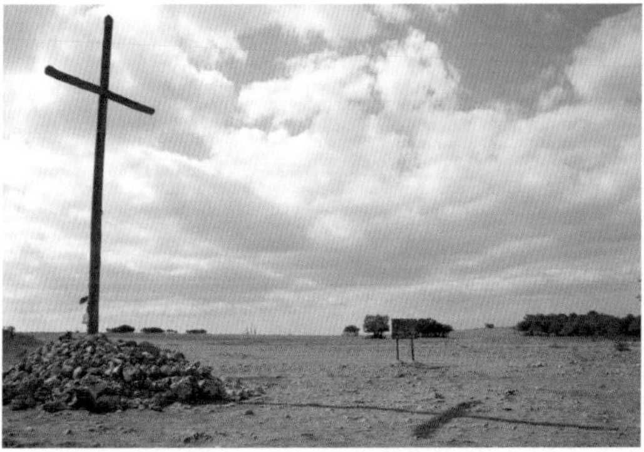

Cross on top of the hill after Atapuerca

3 km to Olmas de Atapuerca

A *Municipal Albergue La Golondrina* (21) c/Iglesia 9 - ♦ 7€. **K.** Closed in Feb and sometimes in Aug. If closed, enquire Bar *Mesón Los Hidalgos*. ☎ 947 430 524. The bar provides sandwiches and ⦿. http://olmosdeatapuerca.wixsite.com/lagolondrina

From the limestone ridge past Atapuerca, shortly after a quarry with a transmitter mast, there is a choice of two routes. Both are waymarked. The southern route has been developed by the Amigos del Camino de Santiago de Burgos, avoiding main roads. Villalval - superb Roman fountain in village 30 m off the camino.

Cardeñuela

A *Bar La Parada-Albergue Municipal de Cardeñuela* (16÷4) c/Santa Eulalia - ♦ 5€. **X 2 weeks in Dec.** ☎ 646 249 597.

Albergue privado Bar Via Minera **PR** (42) - ♦ 5-8€. ⦿ 9€. Bft 2.50€. 3 rooms - bed, breakfast & evening meal 41€. ☎ 652 941 647.

Albergue Santa Fé **PR** (14) c/Los Huertos 2 - ♦ 8+€ B&B. **@. Open all year.** ☎ 626 352 269. www.baralberguesantafe.com.

Orbaneja

A *Albergue Restaurante El Peregrino* (18) c/Principal 1 - ♦ 5€. **Open all year.** ☎ 648 604 577.

Plus a bar and fountain

Villafría (11.5 km from Atapuerca) has several bars and hotels.

The northern route, 1.5 km shorter, follows paths through cornfields (no villages) and the two routes meet just before the flyover crossing the motorway. Here again there are options.

a) In Villafría, cross the Madrid-Irún railway then an 8 km hike into the centre of Burgos along the main N1 (the N1 has broad pavements). Watch out for a crucial turning R before a road junction after about 5 km (at a tall building with a Telefónica sign on top) or you will lose the yellow arrows leading to the route through the centre of the city.

b) A waymarked alternative to the left just after crossing the motorway flyover. No more scenic but much quieter. It meets up with the other route towards the centre of Burgos.

c) Riverpark route: follow b (above) around airport to Castañares, head S to river, pass football ground and cross a blue footbridge.

18 km to Burgos, including 8 km from outskirts (pop 169,682 alt 860 m) 490

Church and Mass - *The Catedral de Santa Maria de Burgos (open 0930-1930). Entry 3.50€ on production of a credencial. Do not wear shorts. Santiago chapel amongst many other attractions. Be cautious with the guides who offer tours in English.* **Mass (no entrance fee) - Daily evening Mass at 19.30, many Masses at other times. www.catedraldeburgos.es. Also Capilla de la Divina Pastora, daily at 19.00 (see Albergue Santiago y Santa Catalina below.)**

Burgos Cathedral

The Catedral de Santa María, the Catedral of Burgos, is a Gothic masterpiece and is arguably one of the finest buildings on the Camino. It is notable for its vast size, magnificent Gothic architecture, and unique history. Burgos Cathedral was added to the World Heritage List in 1984.

The construction of a Cathedral at Burgos was ordered by King Ferdinand III of Castile and Mauricio, the English-born Bishop of Burgos. Construction started on the site of the former Romanesque Cathedral on July 20, 1221.

The high altar was consecrated in 1260, and there was then a lengthy gap of almost 200 years before construction started up again. The Cathedral was finally completed in 1567, with the addition of the spire over the main church.

The architects principally responsible for its construction were a Frenchman named Enrique (who also worked on Leon Cathedral) in the 13th century, and a German named Juan de Colonia in the 15th century. The latter was discovered and hired by the bishop of Burgos while attending the Council of Constance in 1417.

The Cathedral is the burial place of Rodrigo Díaz de Vivar ("El Cid"), and his wife Doña Jimena.

ⓘ Plaza de Alonso Martínez 7 and Plaza del Rey, on the other side of the Cathedral. Mon-Fri 09.00-14.00 & 17.00-19.00. Sat/Sun, 10.00-20.00. Winter closed Saturday pm and Sunday.

A *Municipal Albergue Jacobeo, Casa de los Cubos* (150) c/Fernán González, 28 - ∦ 5€. **Wx2 D** @. Coffee machines and snack dispensers. **Open all year.** 12.00-22.00 (winter), 22.30 (summer). Near the Cathedral. Priority to walking pilgrims.

Albergue Casa Emaús (20÷1) c/San Pedro Cardeña 31b - ∦ 5€. ◖◗ & bft (contribution to cost). Mass and prayer. Pilgrims share in domestic duties. **X All Saints to Easter.** On the way into Burgos by option b (see above), in the La Quinta district as you enter the city, by the side of the Jesuit College at the end of c/Diego Luis Vitores.

Santiago y Santa Catalina (16÷1) c/Laín Calvo 10 (above the Capilla de la Divina Pastora near Cathedral). Walking pilgrims only - ∦ 6€. **W D.** Open 11.00-22.00. **X Dec-Feb.** ☎ 947 207 952.

YH *Residencia Juvenil Gil de Silo* Avda de General Vigón (L off Plaza de Bilbao). Jul-Sep only. YHA Card essential. Meals served.

H *Difficult to find accommodation in late June (fiesta) and July. Try to arrive early in the day and phone ahead if possible. Wide range at all prices.* | *Hostal Conde Miranda* (above bus station) - ∦ 48€. Clean and comfortable. ☎ 947 265 267.

| *Hostal San Juan* Bernabe Pérez Ortiz 1 (Corner of c/Vitoria) - from 40€. ☎ 947 205 134. www.hostalmonjesperegrinos.com. | *Hotel Norte y Londres***, plaza Alonso Martinez. Singles, twins from 30-40€. ☎ 947 264 125. www.hotelnorteylondres.com. *Hotel Centro Los Brasos,* Av. del Cid Campeador, 2 - 🚹 🚹 50€. ☎ 947 252 958. www.hotelcentroburgos.com. | *Hostal riMboMbin* Sombrereria, 6 - 🚹 🚹 50€. ☎ 947 261 200. www.rimbombin.com. With restaurant, close to Cathedral and handy start in morning.

Restaurant *La Gloria* (near *Hospital del Rey*) has an economic *menu.* Restaurant *Rinc*ón de España, between river and Cathedral has been recommended. Also *Gaona, Virgen de la Paloma*. Good places for vegetarians: *Prego* (Italian) 4 Huerto del Rey (near Cathedral); *Mesón de los Infantes* (Cathedral, side of Arco de Santa María); *La Gaia Comedor Vegetariano,* c/San Francisco 31.

The *Museo de Burgos* is worth visiting as is the Church of San Nicolás, near the Cathedral. Burgos was the home of El Cid in the 11th c. See his statue on the Puente de San Pueblo.

⇨ The camino out of Burgos: From the Cathedral follow c/Fernán González, Puerta de San Martín, c/Emperador, c/Villalón and Puente de Malatos.

☞ The *Monasterio de las Huelgas* Museum. Well signposted. Cross Puente de Santa María and turn right, 20 minutes walk. (On turning R, a good red tarmac cycle path on the left goes directly to Hospital del Rey). Apr-Sep. Hours: Tues-Sat 10.00-13.00 and 16.00-17.30; Sun 10.30-14.15. Entrance 7€, includes guided tour (in Spanish). Once one of the most powerful monasteries in Spain. Chapel of Santiago with statue.

The nearby *Hospital del Rey* was an important place of rest for sick or tired pilgrims. 12th -16th c. buildings: see the elaborately carved pilgrims' door and, at the entrance, the Ermita de Santo Amaro, full of relics of people cured of various illnesses. Part of the University campus, the Hospital chapel is open only for Mass. To get there follow the Burgos-Las Huelgas road past a military establishment and follow the wall around the park or take a left fork in the path.

Cartuja de Miraflores, on the eastern outskirts of the city, is still in use as a Carthusian monastery. The church is open (Mon-Sat 10.15-15.00 and 16.00-18.00, Sun 11.20-12.30, 13.00-15.00 and 16.00-18.00). Built 1454-1488, its rich interior reflects its royal patronage.

The altar is plated with the first gold brought back to Spain from America. To get there on foot (45 minutes from the city centre) follow the road east on the south side of the river. The *Cartuja* is on a hilltop. Signposted along c/Valladolid.

☞ **Optional detour to Santo Domingo de Silos** 75 km S. of Burgos. Recommended if time is available. Buses leave Burgos bus station at 17.30 Mon-Thu, 18.30 Fri, 14.00 Sat. Return 08.30. The cloisters are one of the best Romanesque monuments in Spain and include *Christ on the road to Emmaus* showing Jesus dressed as a pilgrim. The Abbey is also world famous for its Gregorian chant. Open Mon-Sat 10.00-13.00 & 16.00-19.00. Sun 12.00-13.00 & 16.00-19.00. 2.40€ plus 0.90€ photo permit. Guided tours only. Last entry 18.00. Mass with Gregorian chant 09.00 (12.00 Sun). Vespers daily at 19.00, Matins 06.00 and Lauds 07.00. Compline 21.30. If travelling by bus or bike you need to stay 2 nights to see Silos properly. Book accommodation in advance. There is no albergue.

H Only men can stay at the monastery. Advance booking essential. ☎ 947 390 049 or 947 390 068. www.abadiadesilos.es. | *Hostal Arco de San Juan,* near the cloister entrance - ♦ 24€. ☎ 947 390 074. | *Hostal Cruces,* Plaza Mayor - ♦ 21€. ♦ ♦ 36€. ☎ 947 390 064. | *H Santo Domingo* - ♦ 22€. ♦ ♦ 30€. ☎ 947 390 053. www.hotelsantodomingodesilos.com.

From Santo Domingo cyclists need not go back to Burgos but can cross to Castrojeriz via Lerma and Santa María del Campo. Lerma is a well preserved hill town with castle of the Dukes of Lerma and all services.

Walkers are advised to buy food in either Burgos or Tardajos.

Cyclists follow N120 out of Burgos to Olmillos de Sasamón. From Olmillos, quiet country roads lead to Hontanas.

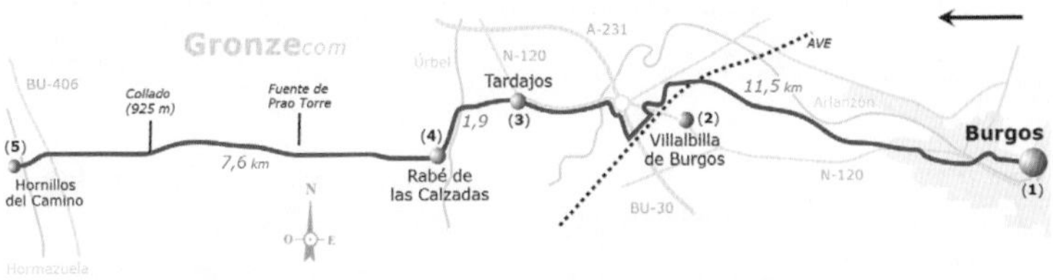

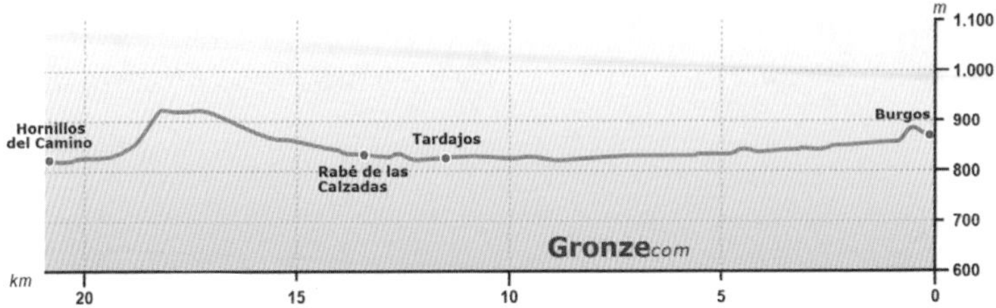

8.5 km to Tardajos 481

A *Albergue Municipal de Tardajos* (16÷3) c/Asunción - *Donativo*. **NK**. **X Nov-Mar**. Ask for the keys at the *Ayuntamiento* from 2 Nov-18 Mar. Open 15.00-22.00. Follow waymarking down a road to the left and keep left. The albergue is on the left and is set back. Run by Madrid Association. *Hospitaleros* are present from 19 Mar-1 Nov.

Albergue La Fábrica **PR** c/de La Fábrica 27 (32) - 🚹 12€. **W D M @. Open all year.** ☎ 646 000 908.

A&H *Casa de Beli* **PR** Albergue (26) avda/General Yagüe 16 - 🚹 10€. **W D @. Open all year.** Hotel - 🚹 (20€). 🚹 🚹 (40€). ☎ 629 351 675. http://lacasadebeli.com

H *Pension Mari-Bar Ruiz* c/Pozas - 🚹 15-20€. 🚹 🚹 20€. 🍽 9.50€. Bft 2.50€. **Open all year**. ☎ 947 451 125.

Another bar, *El Camino*, has sandwiches and snacks and opens for bft at 07.00. Bread shop *Panadería Ordoñez* and two groceries.

1.5 km to Rabé de las Calzadas 479

A *Albergue Liberanos Domine* (24÷4) pl/Francisco Riberas 10 - ♦ 9€. Bft 3€. ◖◗ 8€. **W D. Open all year**. 12.30-22.00. ☎ 695 116 901.

Albergue Santa Marina y Santiago **PR** (8) pl/Francisco Riberas 6 - ♦ 10€. ☎ 670 971 919. www.ospitalsantamarinaysantiago.org

H *Hostal La Fuente de Rabé* c/Santa Marina 17 - ♦ ♦ 40€. ☎ 947 451 191. www.hostalfuentederabe.com

Bar/shop – sandwiches. Open high season from 06.00, low season from 13.00.

8 km to Hornillos del Camino 471

A *Albergue Municipal* (32÷3) pza/de la Iglesia - ♦ 5€. **Open all year.** Until 22.00. **W.** 36 more places in sports hall in summer - showers & mattresses. ☎ 947 411 050. Ask in bar if closed**.**

Albergue El Afar **PR** (20) c/Cantarranas 8 - ♦ 9€. **K M W D @.** ☎ 654 263 857. www.elalfardehornillos.es

Albergue Meeting Point **PR** (36) c/Cantarranas 3 - ♦ 10€. **M W D. Open all year.** ☎ 608 113 599. www.hornillosmeetingpoint.com

H *Casa Rural Sol A Sol* - 16 beds in single and double en suite rooms. ☎ 649 876 091.

La Casa del Abuelo c/Real 44 - ♦ 40€. ♦ ♦ 45€ B&B. ☎ 661 869 618/659 855 326. http://m.lacasadelabuelohornillos.webnode.es.

Bar Casa Manolo, c/Real 16, Menú 10€. Shop in village, 13.00-15.00 & 18.00-21.00; 19/3 - 1/11. Meals and snacks all day at bar.

There is also a Korean Restaurant in Hornillos which offers an interesting Menu of the Day. *Restaurante Wok Ne Son* - Calle San Pedro, 30.

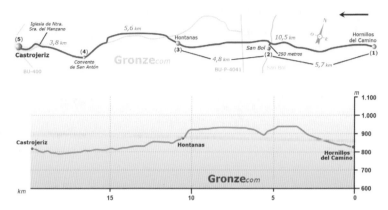

5 km to Arroyo de San Bol 466

A *Municipal Albergue* (12÷1) Basic - 🚹 5€. 🍽 7€. Chapel with a small statue of Christ by the Hungarian Brigitta Járvás.

The spring reputedly has medicinal powers. Pilgrims who washed their feet in it were said to have no further problems with them on the camino.

Wheat fields on the meseta

5 km to Hontanas (alt 750 m) 461

A *Municipal Antiguo Hospital San Juan Peregrino* (55÷2) c/Real - ♪ 6€. Swimming pool. **Open all year.** From 13.00. **K.** 2 overflow buildings (20+ floor space) ☎ 653 243 385.

Albergue Mesón Puntido (40) c/la Iglesia 6 - ♪ 5€. ⦿ 9€. Bft 2€. **W D.** Rooms - ♪ ♪ 25€. Open 11.00-21.00. **X Nov-Feb.** ☎ 947 378 597. Bar open from 06.00 in the summer.

Albergue Santa Brigida, Bar, *Tienda* (16÷3) - ♪ 8€. ⦿ 8€. Bft 2.20€. **W D.** Open 11.00-22.00. **X Nov-Feb.** ☎ 609 164 697. Bar Tienda serves sandwiches and hot dishes from 06.30.

Albergue Juan de Yepes **PR** (54) c/Real 1 - ♪ 7€. **K W D.** ☎ 638 938 546. juandeyepes@santa-brigida.es.

H *Hostal-Restaurante Fuente Estrella*, c/de la Iglesia 6. 7 rooms - ♪ 25-35€. ♪ ♪ 35-45€, bft included. ⦿ 10€. ☎ 947 377 261. www.fuentestrella. com. | *Casa Rural-Restaurante El Descanso*. 8 rooms - ♪ 35€. ♪ ♪ 45€. ⦿ 9€. Bft 2.50€. ☎ 947 377 261. www.casaeldescanso.com. | *Hotel Rural Villa Fontanas* c/Real 23. ♪ 54€. ♪ ♪ 57€. ☎ 680 296 238. www.hotelvillafontanas.com

Swimming pool at the end of the village. Open 15 June to 15 September.

5 km to ruins of the Convent of San Antón 455

A *Albergue San Antón* (14÷1) - *Donativo.* ⦿ & bft. **X Oct-Apr.** Run by volunteer hospitaleros. Despite having no hot water and no electricity the accommodation and toilets are scrupulously clean. Communal evening meal by candlelight. Many pilgrims love staying here.

☞ 14th c. arch stretches across the road. The monks here specialised in caring for pilgrims suffering from 'Saint Antony's fire', a wasting disease caused by a fungus which appeared in Europe in the 10th c. Gangrene was a side-effect. The Antonian monks specialized in amputation. Within the roadway arch are two niches where monks once left bread for travelers who arrived after the gates closed. Pilgrims now leave prayers there. The building was in use from 1146 to 1791.

Ruins of San Antón

4 km to Castrojeriz (pop 904 alt 808 m) 451

Church and Mass - *Convento de Santa Clara Camino de Santa Clara.* **Mass daily at 08.30**. During summer there may be **Mass at 19.00** in the Iglesia de San Juan.

A *Municipal Albergue San Esteban,* Plaza Mayor, in the old Church of St Stephen (35) – 5€**.** Bft available. **NK @. Open all year.** 14.00-22.30. Leave by 08.00. ☎ 947 377 001.

Albergue Casa Nostra **PR** (26÷3) c/Real de Oriente 54 - 🚹 6.50€. Bft 2.50€. **NK W D.** Open 11.00-22.00. **X Dec-Jan.** ☎ 947 377 493.

Albergue Rosalía **PR** (32) c/Cordón 2 - 🚹 10€. **K W D @.** ☎ 947 373 714.

Albergue Ultreia **PR** (28) c/Real de Oriente 77 - 🚹 9€. **W D @.** ☎ 947 378 640.

Albergue Orion **PR** (22÷3) avda/de la Colegiata 28 - 🚹 11€. 🍽10€ - vegan possible. Bft 3€. Private rooms also available - 🚹 30€. 🚹 🚹 40€. 🚹 🚹 🚹 50€. **X 15Dec-15Jan.** ☎ 649 481 609/672 580 959.

Camping-Albergue Casa Rural Camino de Santiago **PR** Albergue (30÷1) - 🚹 16€, including 🍽 & bft.

Albergue A Cien Leguas **PR** c/Real de Oriente 78 - ♦ 10€, plus 5 private rooms from 35€. ⦿ @. ☎ 947 562 305, 619 289 476. info@acienleguas.es. www.acienleguas.es

H *Hostal El Mesón de Castrojeriz* c/Cordón 1 - ♦ 26€. ⦿ 10-14€. ☎ 947 377 400. | *Hotel La Posada* - ♦ 43€. ♦ 64€. ☎ 947 378 610. www.laposadadecastrojeriz.es. |*Hostal Puerta del Monte* - ♦ 21€. ♦ 42€. ⦿ 7.50€. ☎ 947 378 647. www.iacobuscastrojeriz.com. | *La Casa de los Holandeses* c/Real de Oriente 36, a *pension/Casa Rural, La Taberna* at 43, clean and quiet - ♦ 15€. ♦ ♦ 30€. | *Hotel La Cachava*** c/Real de Oriente 93-95. www.hotellacachavacastrojeriz.com

Bar *La Oliva*, near *Albergue de Peregrinos* recommended - @ and ⦿ 7€. *Restaurante Antón* has rooms in a house opposite and late breakfast. Good *panadería*, a *supermercado* and banks.

ⓘ in the *Ayuntamiento*, Plaza Mayor 1. Open May to Sep.

☞ A Roman town, possibly founded by Julius Caesar, built in terraces around a hill. Now visited mainly by pilgrims. A straggling town, it takes about 20 minutes to walk its length. In summer it may be possible to visit three churches on one ticket for 3€. They are Santo Domingo (14thc. Mass 19.00; small museum with a statue of Santa María Peregrina on the upper floor), Santa María del Manzano (13th /17th c. statue of St. James) and San Juan (with a fine cloister). Ruined 13th c. castle on the hill.

Between Castrojeriz and Hospital de San Nicolás you enter the next province of Castile and León, Palencia.

Looking back at Castrojeriz

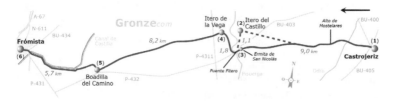

10 km to Hospital de San Nicolás/Itero del Castillo 441

A *Albergue Hospital San Nicolás - Donativo*. Shortly before the Puente Fitero over the Río Pisuerga, in a 13th c. chapel converted by the Italian Confraternity, this albergue offers outstanding hospitality. **Open June to Sept,** 12 beds, supper and bft provided. Open after 15.00. Early arrival essential in July/Aug.

Albergue Municipal de Itero del Castillo (12) c/Sol - ♦ 10€. **B M W @** ☎ 642 213 560. albergueiterocastillo@gmail.com

1 km to Itero de la Vega (pop 310 alt 769 m) 440

A *Albergue Municipal* (13) Plaza Mayor - ♦ 5€. **Open all year**. Key and sello from Bar. A small shop/*restaurante* does meals. ☎ 605 034 347.

Albergue-Hostal-Bar-Rte Tienda Puente Fitero **PR** (22) - ♦ 6€. ♦ 10€. Bft 2.50€. **W D.** Eight rooms - ♦ 30€. ♦ ♦ 40€. ☎ 979 151 822. **Open all year**.

Albergue Bar La Mochila (28) c/Santa Ana - ♦ 6-10€. ♦ 6-8€. Bft 2-3€. **K. Open all day and all year.** ☎ 979 151 781.

Albergue Hogar del Peregrino **PR** (8) c/Santa María 17 - ♦ 12€. **K W D @.** Open all year. ☎ 979 151 866. alberguehogardelperegrino@hotmail.com

☞ Parish church 16th c. chapel at village entrance has St James statue. Shop and bars.

8 km to Boadilla del Camino (pop 268 alt 782 m) 432

A *Albergue En El Camino* **PR** (70÷4) c/Francos 3, *Centro de Turismo Rural* - ⚲ 8€. **NK.** 🍽 9€. Bft 3€. **W**3€ **D**4€ **@. X Nov-Feb.** Private rooms - 35-45€. Swimming pool. ☎ 979 810 284. www.boadilladelcamino.com

Albergue Municipal (12) c/Escuelas - ⚲ 5€. **NK.** Simple. **Open 12.00-22.00 & all year.** ☎ 625 026 677.

Albergue Putzu **PR** (16) c/Las Bodegas 9 - ⚲ 7€. **K W D** ☎ 677 225 993. | *Albergue Titas* **PR** c/Mayor 7 (12) - ⚲ 10€. **M W D @. Open all year.** ☎ 979 810 776. www.alberguetitas.com

H *Hotel En El Camino* c/del Rosario 1 - ⚲ 35€. ⚲ ⚲ 45€. ☎ 979 810 284, 619 105 168. www.boadilladelcamino.com

☞ Church of Santa María with fine Romanesque font. Sole survivor of the 3 churches and 2 pilgrim hospitals which existed here in the 14th century.

Basic shop next to bar. 09.30-14.00 & 16.30-21.00. (**X Sundays**)

The Canal de Castilla begins here, which the Camino follows to Frómista along the tow path.

Canal de Castilla locks near Frómista

6 km to Frómista (pop 1013 alt 780 m) 426

Small town with the Iglesia de San Martín, one of the most perfect Romanesque churches in Spain. Built in 1066, restored c.1900, deconsecrated. The exterior has 315 carved figures (of animals, humans, monsters, flowers etc) stretching all round the exterior at roof level. Open 10.00-14.00 & 16.30-20.00; winter 10.00-14.00 & 15.00-18.30. 1€. Inside are wooden statues of San Martín and Santiago. Other churches are the gothic *Santa María* (near train station, redundant and locked), and *San Pedro*, part of which is a museum of religious art, 11.00-14.00 & 17.30-18.30, **X Mondays.** *Sello* available from *turismo* and also from the parish priest (door marked *Sello* next to restaurant in main square).

Church and Mass - *Iglesia de San Pedro.* **Mass - Tues to Sat at 20.00 (summer), Sun 13.00.**

A *Albergue Municipal de Frómista* (56÷6) plaza de San Martín, near San Martín (see above) - ♦ 8€. Bft 2.50€. **NK. Open all year.** ☎ 979 811 089.

Estrella del Camino **PR** (34÷3) - ♦ 10€. ♦◐8€. Bft 3€. **X Dec-Feb.** ☎ 979 810 399.

Albergue Betania **PR** (5) avda/Ejército Español 26. **Open Dec-Feb** when the other albergues are closed. *Donativo*. Phone ahead ☎ 638 846 043. This albergue is run by Lourdes Lluch, the original Camino hospitalera - she opened the first donativo albergue in a rented house in Hontanas in the early 80s. In winter months she maintains the invaluable webpage that informs pilgrims which accommodations are open and when. http://www.aprinca.com/alberguesinvierno/. | *Albergue Canal de Castilla* **PR** (16) c/La Estación - ♦ 18€. Meal. **W D @.** ☎ 979 810 193. www.albergueperegrinosfromista.com

ⓘ At crossroads in town centre, summer 10.00-14.00 & 16.30-20.00.

H *Hotel San Martín* pza/San Martín 7 - ♦ 38€. ♦ ♦ 50€. www.hotelsanmartin.es. | *Hostal Camino de Santiago* c/Francesa 26. 10 rooms - ♦ 25-34. ♦ ♦ 40-48. Bft 3-4€. ☎ 979 810 053. www.hostalcaminodesantiago.es. | *Hostal Rural Telmo* c/Martín Veña - ♦ 35€. ♦ ♦ 45€. ☎ 979 811 028. www.turismofromista.com/santelmo. | *Hostal San Pedro*** avda/del Ejército Español 8 - ♦ ♦ 50€. ☎ 979 810 016. www.hostalsanpedrodefromista.com

☞ *From Frómista to Carrion de los Condes a broad gravel track,* senda de peregrinos, *has been made for pilgrims.*

Camino Francés 2018/19

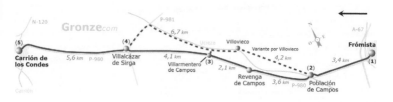

4 km to Población de Campos

A *Albergue Municipal* (18÷1) paseo/del Cementerio - 🛏 5€. **Open all year.**

Albergue La Finca **PR** (20) - 🛏 10€. **W D @. Open all year.** ☎ 979 067 028. www.alberguelafinca.es

H *Hotel Amanecer En Campos* c/Fuente Nueva. 🛏 30€. 🛏 45€. ☎979 811 099, 685 510 020. www.hotelamanecerencampos.com

Also three bars, one with a shop.

Población de Campos has one of the Camino's most fascinating bodega complexes, constructed like an underground village. Uphill behind the Bar Angel on the main street.

⇨ *From Población there are two routes to Villalcázar, one broadly parallel to the river, the other over the bridge along the main road. Both are now well waymarked past Villaviejo (route a).*

a) The route is easy to follow. There is a picnic area and water tap at Villaviejo, also a bar, only open in summer. Continue alongside the river until an arrow left to Villarmentero de Campos. Little shade and water on this route.

b) The road route via Revenga (Church of San Lorenzo, bar and small pensión Casa Vallejera, 3 rooms) and Villarmentero de Campos (San Martín de Tours Church and garden café/bar at entrance to village). Has regular picnic areas with water taps.

A *Albergue Villarmentero de Campos* (20÷2) - 6€. ⏻ 8€. Open 10.00-22.00.

Albergue La Casona de Doña Petra. 12 rooms - ♦ 30€. ♦ ♦ 45€. ⏻ 15€. Bft 5€. ☎ 979 065 978.

Bar Chiringuito serves sandwiches and snacks.

Centro de Turismo Rural.

10 km to Villalcázar de Sirga (pop 209 alt 800 m) 412

The vast 13th c. Gothic church of Santa María la Blanca is a National monument. The Capilla de Santiago has three polychrome tombs and a statue of St James. Opening times vary. 10.30-13.45 & 16.30-19.00 in summer. In winter open to 18.00 & closed Sunday pm. Be sure to illuminate the magnificent retablo.

A *Casa de Peregrinos* (18) Plaza del Palacio - *Donativo.* Hospitaleros from the Amigos de Santiago in Cuenca mid-June to mid-Sept. **K.** Showers - coin in the slot for hot water. Key from *Venta Alcázar* next door, which also does bocadillos. **X Nov-Mar.** ☎ 979 888 041.

Albergue Don Camino **PR** (28) c/Real 23 - ♦ 8€. **W @.** ☎ 979 888 163.

H&A *Albergue/Casas Rurales Aurea y Federico* **PR** (24) Ronda 1&3 - ♦ 8€. **W.** Single and double rooms also available in Casa Rural. ☎ 979 888 163, 620 399 040

H *Hostal las Cántigas.* ☎ 979 888 027. www.hostallascantigas.es. | *Hostal Infanta Doña* - ♦ 30€. ♦ ♦ 40€. ☎ 979 888 018. www.hostal-infantaleonor.com

El Mesón de Villasirga, in a medieval house, is run by the family of one of the characters of the camino, the late D. Pablo Payo. Excellent food ⏻ 14€. Opens 08.30. *Bar Alcázar,* next to the church, is good for bft. Two small shops.

Students walking to Carrión de los Condes

5.5 km to Carrión de los Condes (pop 2534 alt 830 m) 406.5

Now a quiet town with good shops and all facilities, Carrión once had a population of 12,000 and is reputed to be the place where the Moorish overlords required the Christians to surrender 100 virgins every year. The scene is depicted on the portal of Santa María del Camino. The Church of Santiago in the Plaza Mayor has an excellent sculpture above its doorway. There is a small museum attached to this church, open May-Sept, 1€. The *Monasterio de San Zoilo*, at the western end of the town, has a Plateresque cloister and contains the tombs of the counts of Carrión, after whom the town is named. Open 10.30-14.00 & 16.30-19.30. 1€. The monastery itself is now a hotel. There is a Camino Library and Study Centre in the cloister - www.bibliotecajacobea.org. The 13th c. convent of Santa Clara has a museum open Apr-Oct (X Mondays). 10.30-13.30 & 16.30-20.00.

Church and Mass - *Iglesia de Santa María del Camino.* **International Pilgrim Mass at 20.00.**

A *Parish Albergue Santa María* (52) c/Clerigo Pastor, near Church of Santa María - ♦ 5€. **K W D.** Communal meal. Open 12.00-22.00. Leave 06.00-08.00. **X Nov-Feb.** ☎ 979 880 500.

Albergue Espíritu Santo (120) c/San Juan - ♦ 5€. **K. Open all year.** 11.30-22.00. Part of the convent of the Daughters of Charity. Evening Prayer 17.30.

Albergue Nuestra Señora de Belén **PR** (92) Leopoldo María de Castro 6 - ♦ 22€, with meal. **W D. Open all year.** ☎ 979 880 031. www.rfilipenses.com.

H&A *Monasterio de Santa Clara* (30). Beds in smallish rooms - ♦ 5-7€. **K.** Opens 11.00. Rooms with own bathroom in the *hospedería* of the convent - ♦ 22€. ♦ ♦ 44€. **X Dec-Feb.** ☎ 979 880 837. Convent is on route into town, before the church and albergue. A nearby bakery opens at 05.30.

H *Hostal La Corte,* c/Santa María, 16 rooms - ♦ 35-45€. ♦ ♦ 45€. ●◖ 12€. Bft 8€. (Room 103 has an excellent view of the church tympanum). ☎ 979 880 138. www.hostallacorte.com. | *Hotel Monasterio San Zoilo* - ♦ 60€. ♦ ♦ 80€. ☎ 979 880 049. www.sanzoilo.com/es. | *Hostal Santiago* Plaza de los Regentes 8. 16 rooms - ♦ 30-35€. ♦ ♦ 40-45€. ☎ 979 881 052. www.hostalsantiago.es. | *Hostal Albe,* c/Esteban Collantes 21. 8 rooms - ♦ 28€. ♦ ♦ 34€. ☎ 699 094 185. www.hostalalbe.com. | *Apartment Casa Tia Paula* Obispo Souto Vizoso, 8-10 - ♦ €65. ☎ 979 880 331. www.casatiapaula.es.

Hiking Gear: across from Iglesia de Santa María del Camino there is a shop shich sells pilgrim equipment such as boots, shoes and ponchos.

Horse and Carriage: A horse and carriage is available to carry a minimum of 5 pilgrims the 17km stretch from Carrión to Calzadilla. Cost 15€ per person. Leaves at 10am. Reservations: ☎ 867 885 147.

Warning: Please note that there are no services during the 17 kms stretch to Calzadilla de la Cueza and you should ensure you have adequate water and food supplies.

The meseta

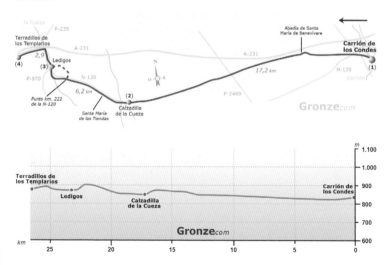

17.5 km to Calzadilla de la Cueza (for walkers on the Calzada de los Peregrinos)

A *Albergue Municipal* (34) c/Mayor 1 - 🚹 5€. **W D V. Open all year.** ☎ 670 558 954.

Albergue Camino Real **PR** (80÷2), on the left at entrance to village - 🚹 5€. **NK @ W D**. Swimming pool. **Open all year.** ☎ 979 883 187.

H Hostal Camino Real, 26 rooms - 🚹 30€. 🚹 🚹 45€. 🍽 10€. Bft 3€. **@**. Bar opens for bft. **X Dec-Jan.** ☎ 979 883 187.

1 km after Calzadilla you are at the half-way point between Saint-Jean and Santiago.

6 km to Ledigos (147; 863 m) 383

A *Albergue El Palomar* **PR** (52÷7) c/Ronda de Abajo 4 - 🚹 6-7€. 🍽 9€. Bft 2.50€. Bike storage. **K W @.** Five rooms - 🚹 🚹 18€ pp. ☎ 979 883 614/979 883 605. Key from adjacent bar which runs the albergue. It also has a shop and serves a Pilgrim *menú* 7.50€. **X Jan-Feb**.

A&H *Albergue La Morena* **PR** (37) c/Carretera 3 - 🚹 8€. **W @.** Also 9 single, double and triple rooms - 🚹 🚹 30€. **Open all year.** ☎ 655 877 305. www.alberguelamorena.com

The 13th c. church dedicated to Santiago has 3 different statues of Saint James.

3 km to Terradillos de los Templarios 380

A *Albergue-bar-Restaurante Jacques de Molay* **PR** (49÷9) c/de la Iglesia, next to No 18 - 🚹 8-10€. 🍽 10€. Bft 3€. **NK.** Food shop. More basic accommodation in the attic for overflow (30), no sheets or blankets - 🚹 4€. **Open all year**. ☎ 979 883 679.

Albergue Los Templarios **PR** (52÷6) - 🚹 8-10€. 🍽 10€. Bft 3€. Laundry facilities. Bike storage. **@. X Dec-Feb**. On the left at the start of the village. ☎ 979 883 679

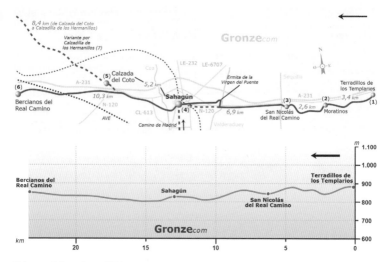

3 km to Moratinos 377

A *Albergue Bar Restaurante Hospital San Bruno* (32) c/Ontanon 9 - 🕯 7-9€. 🍽 9.50-12€. Bft 3€. Two rooms - 🕯 25€. 🕯 🕯 32€. **W. X Feb-Mar**. ☎ 979 061 465.

H&A *Hostal Restaurante Moratinos* c/Real 12. Albergue - dorms of 4 beds - 10€. Hostal - 🕯 30-40€. 🕯 🕯 40-50€. Bft 3€. 🍽 12.50€. Jacuzzi. **X Dec-Feb** ☎ 979 061 466.

At c/Ontanon 2, Rebekah Scott and Patrick O'Gara offer refreshment to passing pilgrims, emergency shelter if someone is exhausted, other emergency assistance and overnight hospitality to up to 3 pilgrims. ☎ 648 539 188, 979 061 016. rebrites@yahoo.com

Bar restaurant El Castillo de Moratinos. Closed Jan and Feb on the route through Moratinos just before the church.

3 km to San Nicolás del Real Camino 374

R *Albergue Laganares* (22) - 🕯 9€. 🍽 10€. Bft 2.50€. **W D.** One room - 🕯 🕯 30€. ☎ 629 181 536.

H *Bar-Rte Casa Barrunta* (also rents rooms) serves meals/bft. Very famous for excellent paella. Rooms and paella should be reserved in advance. ☎ 689 336 189.

There is a small grocery store near the *Albergue Laganares.* Summer only.

The brick church is typical of the area, built by Moorish craftsmen who stayed on after the reconquest, in the style which became known as *mudéjar.*

Soon after San Nicolás you leave Palencia and enter León.

7.5 km to Sahagún (pop 3,351 alt 816 m) 366.5

The approach to this ancient town is discouraging. It was once the seat of the largest, most powerful Benedictine Monastery in Spain. All that remains of that now is a huge arch of the gateway and belfry, which requires a slight detour as you arrive. Also there are the 12th c churches of *San Lorenzo* (open 10.00-14.00, 16.00-20.00; closed Monday & Thursday) and *San Tirso*, in *mudéjar* style (open summer Tues/Sat 10.30-13.30 & 17.00-20.00, Sun 10.00-15.00; and winter Tues/Sat 10.30-13.30 & 16.00-19.00, Sun 10.30-13.30). Near *San Tirso* is *La Peregrina*, the remains of a *mudéjar* monastery and a restored 13th c. chapel. Through the archway of *San Tirso* is the *Monasterio Santa Cruz,* where the nuns have an interesting museum of religious art. Open 10.30-12.30 & 16.00-18.30.

Archway of San Tirso, Sahagún

Camino Francés 2018/19

Church and Mass - *Monasterio de Santa Cruz (Benedictinas).* **Mass daily 08.30, Sun 09.00. Vespers Daily at 19.00 - pilgrims invited.**

A *Monasterio de la Santa Cruz* (50) c/Antonio Nicolas 40. Operated by the Marist Fathers - ♦ 5€. Rooms are of 4 people (one of 6) and there is also possibility of double/individual rooms. Each room is en-suite with full bathroom. Kitchen, chapel, dining-room, sitting-room, Wifi, washer machine (3€), hot water and central heating. They also welcome groups and cyclists. Communal dinner at 20:00h; they also have a gathering with the pilgrims to share experiences in the afternoon (17:00h) and Mass (18:30h) and pilgrims' blessing (19:00h). ☎650 696 023. alberguesantacruzsahagun@gmail.com. www.alberguesensahagun.es

Albergue Municipal Cluny (64) - ♦ 5€. **K. Open all year.** 12.00-22.30 prompt. Leave 08.30. *Credenciales* available. ☎ 987 781 015. Built into the upper levels of the restored Church of *La Trinidad* in the town centre above the ⓘ, which will provide a map of the town. St James statue outside.

Albergue El Labriego **PR** (19) av/Bermejo y Calderón 9 - ♦ 8€. ☎ 722 115 161.

A&H *Albergue-Hostal Domus Viatoris* **PR** (50÷6) Travesia del Arco 25 - ♦ 5-7€. ▯◖ 10€. bft 3€. **K W @.** Bike repair. 19 rooms - ♦ 20-27€. ♦ 35-45€. **Open all year.** ☎ 987 780 975.

H *Hostal Escarcha* c/Regina Franco 12 - ♦ 20€. ♦ 30€. ☎ 987 781 856. www.hostalescarcha.com. | *Hostal La Cordorniz, c/Arco,* top of the town near the station - ♦ 40€. ♦ 50€. ☎ 987 780 276. www.hostallacodorniz.com. | *Hotel Las Balcones del Camino* Calle Juan Guaza 2 - ♦ 35€. ♦ ♦ 45€. ☎ 676 838 242. www.losbalconesdelcamino.es. | *La Bastide du Chemin* c/del Arco 66 - ♦ 28€. ♦ ♦ 40€. ☎ 987 781 183. www.labastideduchemin.es. | *Hostal Pacho* Constitución 84 - ♦ ♦ 35€. ☎ 987 780 775. www.hostalpacho.com. | *Hotel Puerta de Sahagún* c/Burgos - ♦ 60€. ♦ 90€. ☎ 987 781 880. www.hotelpuertadesahagun.es

Several restaurants, *farmacias* and a *zapatería* which sells sports shoes. There are also two shops selling shoes, boots, backpacks, as well as repairs and resupplying camping and outdoors gear.

⇨ **From Sahagún cyclists take the N120, now a pleasant road with only light traffic.**

4.5 km to Calzada del Coto 362.5

A *Albergue Municipal San Roque* (36÷2) c/Real - *Donativo*. **NK @. Open all day & all year.** ☎ 987 784 008. Key from Maxi at c/Mayor 4.

The Bar/Restaurant *Estebuca* in town does meals. There is also a small unmarked shop.

⇨ 300 metres before Calzada there is a choice of two routes: the *real Camino Francés*, suitable for walkers and cyclists; and the *Calzada de los Peregrinos*, only for walkers. The choice has to be made at the point where the new bridge goes over the motorway. To follow the *Real Camino* do not cross the bridge but keep straight on. Crossing the bridge will bring you to Calzada del Coto and the other route.

Real Camino Francés route. *The camino consists of a 2 m wide gravel path. Trees have been planted to provide shade.*

5.5 km to Bercianos de Real Camino 357

A *Parish Albergue Casa Rectoral* (46÷6) c/Santa Rita 11 - *Donativo*. Meals. Open all day. **X Nov-Mar.**

Albergue Santa Clara **PR** (8) - ♦ 8€. **K W D @. Open all year.** ☎ 605 839 993.

Albergue Bercianos 1900 **PR** (20÷2) c/Mayor 49 - ♦ 15-25€. **K W D @.** ☎ 669 282 824, 987 784 244. hello@bercianos1900.com. www.bercianos1900.com.

Albergue La Perla **PR** Camino Sahagún. (58) ♦ 10€, also has rooms. ☎ 685 817 699. alberguelaperala@hotmail.com.

H *Hostal- Rte Rivero* c/Mayor 12. 8 rooms - ♦ 30-35€. ♦ 40-45€. ⏹ 10€. ☎ 987 784 287. www.hostalrivero99.wixsite.com/hostal-rivero-. | *Alojamiento El Sueve* c/La Iglesia 21. ♦ 30€. ♦ 45€. ☎ 987 784 139, 625 322 021.

Two shops. ☞ Church of El Salvador.

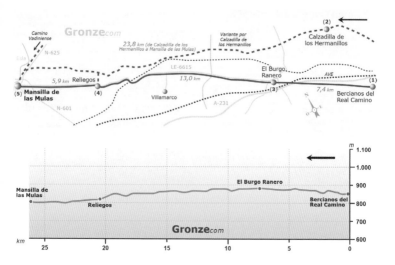

8 km to El Burgo Ranero 349

A *Albergue Municipal Domenico Laffi* (28) - *Donativo*. **K W D. Open all year.** 13.00-22.00. Association hostel run by volunteers. ☎ 987 330 047. Brown adobe house between Plaza Mayor and Sports court. If closed get key from *Tienda Pili.*

Albergue El Nogal **PR** (30) c/Fray Pedro 42 - ╫ 7€. **X Oct-Easter.** ☎ 627 229 331.

Albergue La Laguna **PR** (18) c/La Laguna 12 - ╫ 9 -12 € also rooms. ║◉║ ☎ 603178627

A&H *Hostal Rural-Bar Piedras Blancas/Albergue La Laguna* (24) - ╫ 8€. ║◉║ 10€. **K.** Bungalows for 2 people - ╫ 12€. 16 rooms - ╫ 30€. ╫ ╫ 45€. **Open all year.** From 05.00. ☎ 987 330 094. www.hotelruralpiedrasblancas.com

H *Hostal-Bar-Restaurante Peregrino* (10) Ic/Fray Pedro 32. Ten rooms - ╫ 30€. ╫ ╫ 45€, including bft. ║◉║ 10€. **W. Open all year. F**rom 05.00. ☎ 987 330 069. | *Hotel-Restaurante Castillo El Burgo-Station.* Ten rooms - ╫ 33€. ╫ ╫ 53€, including bft. ║◉║ 10.50-13€. **Open all year, 24/7.** ☎ 987 330 403. www. hotelcastilloelburgo.com

Two shops, one near to Albergue Domenico Laffi. *Farmacia.*

13 km to Reliegos 330

A *Municipal Albergue Don Gaiferos* (44) c/Escuelas 2 - ⫟ 5€. **K. Open all year.** 12.00-22.30. If the albergue is closed ask at No 13 c/Escuelas for the keys. ☎ 686 527 505.

Albergue-Bar La Parada **PR** (36÷6) c/Escuelas 7 - ⫟ 7€. **K.** ⫠ 10€. Two rooms - ⫟ ⫟ 30€. **X Christmas & low season.** ☎ 987 317 880.

Albergue-Bar-Restaurante Piedras Blancas II **PR** (9) - ⫟ 9€. 2 rooms - ⫟ 30€. ⫟ ⫟ 40-45€. ⫠ 10€. Bft 3€. **X Nov-Feb.** ☎ 607 163 982.

Bar Gil I and Gil II **PR** (6) c/Cantas, 28 - ⫟ 8€. ⫠ 9€. 2 rooms - ⫟ ⫟ 30€. Bft at the bar Gil II. Open from 07.30. ☎ 987 317 804.

Albergue Ada PR c /Real 2 (20) - ⫟ 8€. ⫠ (vegetarian) 9€. Bft 4€. **N M W D @.** ☎ 691 153 010. www.alberguereliegos.es.

Albergue Vive Tu Camino **PR** (20÷2) c/Real 56 - ⫟ 9€. ⫠ 9€. **M W D @.** ☎ 610 293 986, 670 885 959. carmenmagin@gmail.com. www.alberguevivetucamino.com

Bar La Torre (also known as the Bar Elvis!) Plaza La Barrera serves hot meals. www.templete.org/2013/06/el-bar-de-elvis-en-reliegos-famoso-en.html.

The church is open all day in summer.

6 km to Mansilla de las Mulas (details follow after route description)   **330**

Calzada de los Peregrinos route.

Walkers who prefer a more authentic, mainly Roman way to Mansilla, and who are fit, may like to take this route, also known as the *Calzada Romana* or the *Via Trajana*. It is not suitable for bikes. Little shelter or shade and no water or food between Calzadilla and Mansilla.

⇨ *To join it, turn right over the bridge into Calzado del Coto.*

9 km to Calzadilla de los Hermanillos (from Calzada)

A *Albergue de San Bartolomé* (26) - *Donativo*. Bunks. **K W/D** (coin operated). Basic and clean. Good reports. ☎ 987 330 023. www.aytoelburgoranero.es

Albergue-Restaurante-Bar Via Trajana **PR** 3 rooms, 2-4 people - ♀ 15€. 5 dbl rooms - ♀♀ 35€. Bft from 07.00 3€. 🍽 10€. **W D. X Nov-Feb.** ☎ 987 337 610/600 220 104.

H *Restaurante-Casa de Comidas Via Trajana* opens 07.00 Easter to October. Good pilgrim *menú* 10€. Bft 3-5€. 2 bars, one with food (in summer). Shop in a side street, about 400 m from *albergue*. Fountain in front of *albergue*.

22 km to Mansilla de las Mulas across *meseta*. Railway halt of Villamarcos (not in use) c 12 km.

Mansilla de las Mulas (pop 1800 alt 799 m) 330

Mansilla de la Mulas

Church and Mass - *Iglesia de Santa Maria. On the site of the first and only church in Mansilla de las Mullas until the 13th c. The current Church of Santa Maria was built in the 18th c.* **Mass daily at 08.30 and Vespers at 20.30.**

A *Albergue Municipal Laura Barredo* (68÷7) c/del Puente 15 - ✝ 5€. **W D K @.** Bike storage. Extra mattresses on floor. Open 12.00-23.00. **X Dec-Feb.** ☎ 661 977 305

Albergue-Restaurante-Bar El Jardin del Camino **PR** (32÷2) c/Camino de Santiago 1 - ✝ 5-10€ (10€ in winter). ⦿ 10€. Bft 3.50€. ☎ 987 310 232.

Albergue Gaia **PR** (18) av/de la Constitución 28 - ✝ 5+€. **K W D @. Open all year.** ☎ 699 911 311. www.alberguedegaia.wordpress.com.

H *Pensión de Blanca* av/Picos de Europa. Seven Rooms - ✝ 25-35€. ✝ 40€.

Albergueria del Camino, 4 rooms - ✝ 38€. ✝ 56€. ⦿ 10€. Bft 4€. ☎ 987 311 193 (**NOTE:** This is not the albergue).

Casa Rural – La Casa de los Soportales, next door to the albergue - ✝ 30 -35€. ✝ ✝ 40-50€. ☎ 987 310 232. www.albergueeljardindelcamino.com/la-casa-de-los-soportales.

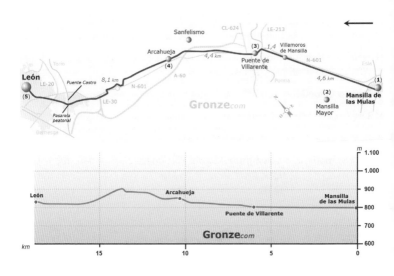

6 km to Puente de Villarente (alt 804 m) 324

Camino Francés 2018/19

A *Albergue San Pelayo* **PR** (64÷4) c/El Romero 9 - ♦ 8€ (10€ in winter). ⏺
10€. Bft 3€. **K.** 6 rooms - ♦ 30€. ♦ ♦ 40€. **@.** Bike storage. **Open all year.** 12.00-
22.00. Book in low season. ☎ 987 312 677. After crossing the bridge, follow
yellow arrows on the right side of the road that lead to a side road about half
way through the village.

Albergue El Delfín Verde **PR** (20÷3) - ♦ 5€. ⏺ 10€. Plus 15 rooms - ♦ 25€. ♦ ♦ 40€,
bft included. Swimming pool in summer. **X Dec-Feb.** ☎ 987 312 065.

H *Hostal La Montaña,* 16 rooms - ♦ 27€. ♦ ♦ 45€. ⏺ 10-15€. **Open all year.** ☎
987 312 161. www.hostalrestaurantelamontana.es.

⇨ After the village look out for *Bar Aveñalleda*, after the Repsol petrol station,
where walkers turn right for the off road path.

4 km to Arcahueja 320

A&H *Bar Restaurante Albergue La Torre* (22÷2) - ♦ 10€. ⏺ 9€. Bft 3€. **W D.** 4
rooms - ♦ 25-35€. ♦ ♦ 25-40€. **Open all year.** Call ahead Mar-Nov. ☎ 987 205
896/669 660 914. Beside the church. www.alberguetorre.es

H *Hotel Restaurante Camino Real.* 44 rooms - ♦ ♦ 65€. Bft 2.60-4.70€. ⏺
12.50-18€. **Open all year.** ☎ 987 218 134.

1.5 km to Valdelafuente

H Bar/Rte *Santa Fe* is 200 m further on the main road.

6.5 km to León (pop 147,625 alt 822 m) 312

⇨ *Follow main road down from Alto del Portillo for 1 km; where the bypass
swings away to the right, keep straight on into Puente Castro. Cross the Río
Torio by the footbridge. There may be an open information kiosk as you walk
into León.*

⇨ *To reach the municipal albergue: after crossing the footbridge go along
c/Alcalde Miguel Castaño, turn left into Avda Fernández Ladrera, Left again
into c/Monseñor Turrado, alongside the Guardia Civil Barracks, and so into c/
Campos Góticos. The albergue is across the road.*

The fourth large city on the route and a major highlight. The main sights to
see follow.

The Cathedral of *Santa María de León* is also called the House of Light or the *Pulchra Leonin*. The Cathedral was built on the site of 2nd century Roman baths. Almost all of the Cathedral was built between 1205 and 1301. The north tower and cloister were built in the 14th century, and the south tower was completed in 1472.

The Cathedral, which is dedicated to Santa María de la Regla, was declared of Cultural Interest in 1844. The building is a masterpiece of the Gothic style of the mid13-th century. The design is attributed to the architect Enrique. By the mid 15th century the building was virtually completed.

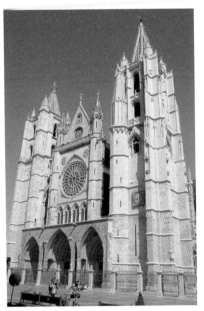

León Cathedral

The main façade has two towers. The southern tower is known as the 'clock tower'. The Renaissance retrochoir contains alabaster sculptures by Jusquin, Copin of Holland and Juan de Malinas. Particularly noteworthy is the Plateresque iron grill work screen in the wall behind the sepulchre of King Ordoño.

Camino Francés 2018/19

It has three portals decorated with sculptures situated in the pointed arches between the two towers. The central section has a large rose window. Particularly outstanding is the image of the *Virgen Blanca* and the *Locus Appellatione*.

The Cathedral has nearly 1,800 square metres of stained glass windows. The great majority of them date from the thirteenth to the fifteenth centuries: a rarity among medieval gothic churches.

In the main chapel, there is an altarpiece by Nicolás Francés (15th century) and a silver urn containing the relics of *San Froilán*, the town's patron saint, made by Enrique de Arfe. The 13th- to 15th-century cloister contains sculpted details in the capitals, friezes and ledges.

The Cathedral Museum houses a large collection of sacred art. There are almost 1,500 pieces, including 50 Romanesque sculptures of the Virgin, dating from pre-historic times to the 18th century (Neoclassicism) with works by Juan de Juni, Gregorio Fernández, Mateo Cerezo, a triptych of the School of Antwerp, a Mozarabic bible and numerous codices. The first manuscript in Leonese language, the Nodicia de Kesos, can be found in its archives.

Leon Cathedral is also one of the three most important Cathedrals in Spain, along with that of Burgos and Santiago de Compostela.

Visits to the Cathedral: daily 09.30h-13.30h and 16.00h-19.00h. Ticket to museum, cloisters, chapter house etc. 5€. Cloister only, 1€. *Sello* from the museum.

The *Basilica of San Isidoro*, 12th c, open all day, was a compulsory halt for pilgrims. Outside is the *Puerta del Perdón*. The bones of the Saint are in a reliquary on the high altar. A separate entrance on the main façade leads into the 11th c *Pantheon*, one of the oldest Romanesque buildings, now the *museo*. Vivid 12th c wall and ceiling paintings. Good bookshop. WCs in basement. Open daily 10.00-13.30 & 16.00-18.30, Sun 10.00-13.30. 3€.

***San Marcos*.** 12th c. monastery for the Knights of Santiago, rebuilt in the 16th c as their headquarters. The huge façade, Romanesque/Plateresque, has a *Santiago Matamoros*. Now a luxury hotel, it will provide a *sello* even to non-residents.

Adjacent is the ***Iglesia San Marcos***. A museum in the sacristy is open Tues-Sat, 10.00-14.00 & 17.00-19.30; Sun 10.00-14.00. The original two-storey pilgrim hospital, next to the hotel, is now used by the legal services of *Castilla y León*.

The **church of *Santa María del Mercado*** (formerly *'del Camino'*) is evocative of the camino and the medieval pilgrimage.

Church and Mass - *Catedral de Santa María de León.* **Mass daily every hour from 09.00 - 14.00 & 18.00.** *Basílica de La Virgen del Camino (Dominicans).* **Mass daily 08.30 and 18.30 - pilgrims particularly welcome.**

A *Albergue San Francisco* (144÷24) av/Alcade Miguel Castaños 4 - ♱ 10€. 13 rooms - ♱ ♱ 30€. Bft. ☻. **W D @.** Bike store. **Open all year.** ☎ 987 215 060.

Albergue Check in León **PR** (40) av/Alcalde Miguel Castaños 88 - ♱ 10€. **K W D @. Open all year.** ☎ 987 498 793. www.checkinleon.com

Albergue Leon Hostel **PR** (14) c/Ancha 8 - ♱ 12€. **K @. Open all year.** ☎ 987 079 907.

Albergue Muralla Leonesa **PR** (65) c/Tarifa 5 - ♱ 10€. **W D @. Open all year.** ☎ 987 177 873. www.alberguemurallaleonesa.com

Albergue Santo Tomás de Canterbury **PR** (54) av/de La Lastra 53 - ♱ 8€. **K W D @.** ☎ 987 392 626. www.alberguesantotomas.com

Albergue Unamuno **PR** (86) c/San Pelayo 15 - ♱ 10€. **W D @.** ☎ 987 233 010. www.residenciaunamuno.com/albergue2/en

Albergue Urban Río Cea **PR** (8) c/Legion VII - ♱ 18 B&B. **K W D @. Open all year.** ☎ 639 179 386. www.hostelurbanriocea.com

A&H *Albergue Convento Santa María de las Carbajalas* (140÷4), c/de Escurial/plaza de Santa María del Camino - ♱ 5€, in segregated male/female dorms. **W**3€ **D**3€. Secure bike storage. *Credencial* available. Also 25 rooms in the Hospedería Antigua - ♱ ♱ 49-100€. ♱ single supplement 16.50€. ☻ 9-25€. Bft 8€. **Open all Year.** 11.00-21.30. Leave 08.00. ☎ 680 649 289. Vespers 19.00. Compline 21.45. Pilgrims may attend. | **H** Some suggestions. *León Hostel,* C/Ancha 8-3 - ♱ ♱ 28€. ♱ ♱ ♱ 13€ each. ☎ 987 079 907. www.leonhostel.es/en. | *Hostal Bayón,* c/AlcazarToledo 6 - ♱ 23€. ☎ 987 231 446. | *Hospedería Fernando* avda/Los Cubos 32 - 50€ double. ☎ 987 220 731. www.hospederiafernandoi.com/hospederia.htm. | *Hostal Casco Antiguo* c/Cardenal Landarzuri 11 - ♱ ♱ 35-50€. ☎ 987 074 000. | *Hostal Don Suero* Avda Suero de Quiñones 15 - ♱ 24€. ♱ ♱ 40€. Between San Isidoro and San Marcos. ☎

987 230 600. www.hostaldonsuero.es. | *Pensión Sandoval* Pza San Francisco 19, entrance in c/Hospicio - ♦ 20-35€. ♦ ♦ 35-50€. ☎ 987 212 041. On the route. www.pensionsandovalleon.com. | *Hostal Alvarez* c/Burgo Nuevo - ♦ ♦ 40€. Recommended for cyclists - ask about bike storage. ☎ 987 072 520. | *Hotel Paris* c/Ancha 20, near Cathedral - ♦ 50-80€. ☎ 987 238 600. www.hotelparisleon.com. | *Hotel FC Infantas León* González de Lama 3 - ♦ 60€. ☎ 987 272 317. www.hotelinfantasdeleon.com. | *Hospederia Pax* Plaza de Santa María del Camino 11 - ♦ ♦ 40-60€. ☎ 987 344 493. www.hospederiapax.com

This is not a full listing. For more possibilities, visit the tourist office in Plaza Regla, opposite the Cathedral, or www.booking.com

Casa Botines

⇨ *Camino through León: Church of Santa Ana, c/Barahona, Puertamoneda, Santa María del Mercado, c/Rua, Ancha, Catedral, Sierra Pambley, Damaso Merino, Cervantes, Plaza Torres de Omaña, Fernando Reguero, San Isidoro, turn right along walls of San Isidoro (Avda Ramon y Cajal), then left along Renueva, Suero de Quiñones, San Marcos and then over the bridge. Go straight on. Soon after the Chapel of Santiago (on the right) there is a yellow arrow to the left taking you through new housing and then a polígono (an industrial estate). You emerge on the main N120 shortly before Virgen del Camino.*

4 km Trobajo del Camino 300

H *Hostal El Abuelo* c/Los Mesones 6 - 🚹 35€. 🚹 50€. ☎ 987 801 044. www. hostalelabuelo.es. | *Hotel Alfageme* c/de las Lagunas 1. 🚹 48€. 🚹 🚹 55€. ☎ 987 840 490. www.hotelalfageme.es.

7 km to Virgen del Camino (pop 3300 alt 906 m) 304

A small town dating back to the 10th c. There is a modern church to the right of the route. The statues of the apostles on the façade include St. James, pointing the way to Santiago. Friendly Dominican priests have a *sello* and may offer a tour of the church.

A *Albergue Municipal D Antonino y Dña Cinia* (40÷2) - 🚹 6€. **W**2€ **D**2€. **K.** Comfortable, warm and well equipped. Opens 12.00-23.00. **X Nov-Feb.** ☎ 987 302 800. Signed from the N120.

H *Hostal Julio César & Bar Pablo.* 8 rooms - 🚹 25€. 🚹 🚹 40€. 🍽 10€. Bft 3-4€. ☎ 987 302 044. Follow *Camas* signs. | *Pensión Soto* - 🚹 24-30€. **Open all year.** ☎ 987 802 925. www.hostalsoto.es | *Hostal-Restaurante Central.* 29 rooms - 🚹 20€. 🚹 🚹 40€. 🍽 10€. Bft 3.50€. ☎ 987 302 041. www.hostalrestaurantecentral.com

Camino Francés 2018/19

Many bars and restaurants.

⇨ *Just after Virgen del Camino, there is a choice of route, as shown by yellow markers on the road surface and a map on a post. The traditional route follows the main road with the hazards and noise of modern traffic. The other is quieter, but slightly longer. For ease of reference they are here called The Road Route and The Walkers Route (but OK for cyclists as well). Both are fully waymarked.*

Road route to Hospital de Orbigo (24 km)

3 km to Valverde de la Virgen 301

A *Albergue la Casa del Camino* **PR** (32) Camino El Jano 2 - ⭑ 8€. **Meals. W D @.** ☎ 987 303 455/669 874 750. www.alberguelacasadelcamino.com.

H Rte *El Yugo,* at the end of the village. A pleasant friendly bar.

1 km to San Miguel del Camino 300

H Bar/Mesón *El Rincón de Julia* c/de la Fuente. Friendly. *Panadería* and a cash machine.

7 km to Villadangos del Páramo 294

A *Albergue Municipal de Villadangos* (54) - ⭑ 7€. **K W D** (coins needed). **Open all year.** 11.30-22.00. ☎ 987 102 910. A *panadería* on the right on the route out of the village also has a *sello.*

H *Hostal-Rte Avenida III* (65 rooms) - ⭑ 35€. ⭑ ⭑ 40-48€. 🍽 12€. Bft 3€. **Open all year.** ☎ 987 390 151. www.hotelavenidaiii.com/en/. | *Hostal Bar Restaurante Libertad* c/Padre Angel Martinez Fuertes 25. 24 rooms - ⭑ 35€. ⭑ ⭑ 45€. 🍽 12-14€. **X Sat and Christmas.** ☎ 987 390 123.

Campsites: *Camping Camino de Santiago* Cat 2. N120, km 324. Tent for two 16€. **W.** Pool. **X Oct-Feb.**

5 km to San Martin del Camino

A *Albergue de la Junta Vecinal* (60) - ⭑ 5€. **K.** Close to the water tower on the right hand side of the road.

A&H *Albergue Santa Ana* **PR** (40÷2) - 6€. 9€. Bft 3€. Sandwiches. **K W D.** 12 rooms - 20€. **Open all year.** ☎ 987 378 653.

Albergue Vieira (40) - 7€. 10€. Bft 4€. **K W. Open all year.** ☎ 987 378 565.

Albergue La Casa Verde **PR** San Martín del Camino (8) - 10€ B&B. **K W D @.** ☎ 646 879 437. alberguelacasaverde@gmail.com.

2 bars, baker (closed Sunday). Shop - open Sunday morning. Health centre ☎ 987 378 663.

⇨ After San Martín, the route follows the road until a right turn to Hospital de Orbigo (7 km).

Walkers route to Hospital de Orbigo (26.5 km)

⇨ Turn left off the road as indicated by waymarking about 100 m before the flyover. Follow the road signs which indicate the route. Head first for Fresno del Camino (road signs indicating *'Camino de Santiago'* will take you back to the N120).

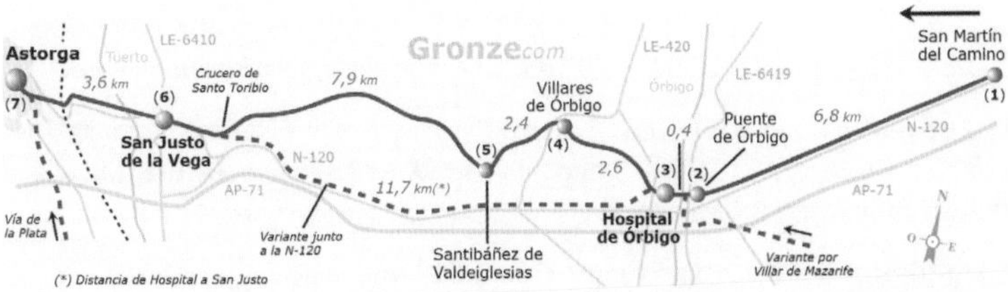

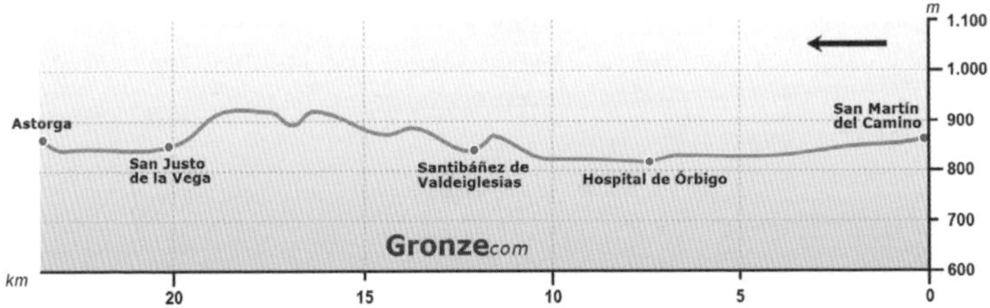

3.5 km to Oncina 305

Small village, no facilities, water tap.

5.5 km to Chozas de Abajo 300

One bar (off the camino), open Sunday morning, serves bocadillos.

4 km to Villar de Mazarife 296

A *Albergue Paraíso de Jesús* **PR** (50÷6) c/Corujo 11 - ♦ 5€. ⦿ 9€. Bft 2.50-3€. **K W D. Open all day and all year.** ☎ 987 390 697.

Albergue San Antonio de Padua **PR** (52÷1) c/León 33 - ♦ 8-10€. ⦿ (vegetarian) 9€. Bft 4€. **W D.** Five rooms - ♦ ♦ 30-50€. **Open all year.** From 05.30 (in summer). ☎ 987 390 192.

Albergue–Restaurante-Bar Tio Pepe **PR** (20÷4) c/El Teso de la Iglesia 2 - ♦ 9€. ⦿ 9€. Bft 3€ (from 07.00). Also 10 rooms - ♦ ♦ 40-50€, bft included. Open 06.30-23.00. **X Dec-Feb,** and Tuesday in low season. ☎ 987 390 517.

H *Mesón Rosy*. Open from 06.00. Sandwiches and hot meals, *Cocido* 8.50€. 2 shops, 2 bars and a baker.

9.5 km to Villavante 286

A *Albergue Santa Lucía* (28) c/Doctor Velez 17 - ♦ 9€. ⦿ 8.50€. Bft 3.50€. 3 rooms - ♦ ♦ 20-40€. ☎ 987 389 105. alberguesantalucia@hotmail.com.

H *Casa Rural Molino Galochas*, 6 rooms - ♦ 35€. ♦ ♦ 55€, bft included. ⦿ 15€. Bungalow 4-5 pers - ♦ 20€. **K. Open all year**. ☎ 987 388 546. By the side of the railway on leaving the village.

4 km to Hospital de Orbigo (pop 1320 alt 819 m)

The main claim to fame of the town, also known as Puente de Orbigo, is the Bridge of the *Paso Honroso* - 20 arches, 204 m long and one of the oldest in Spain. Walkers and cyclists (but not motorists) enter the town over this bridge. The "Hospital" in the name was a pilgrim hospital founded by the Knights of Saint John of Jerusalem.

Hospital del Órbigo

Church and Mass - *Iglesia de Santa Maria,* facing the bridge. **Mass for pilgrims at 20.00. Sun 12.00.**

A *Albergue Parochial Karl-Leisner* (100) c/Alvarez Vega 32 - �pilgrim 5€. **K**. Limited showers and toilets. **Open all day and all year.** ☎ 987 388 444. Go west 50 m beyond the church. A historic building with a central courtyard.

Albergue San Miguel (36÷5) c/Alvarez Vega - �pilgrim 7-10€. Bft (from 06.00) 3€. **W**3€ **D**3€ **@.** Hot drinks machine. Open 11.00-22.30. ☎ 987 388 285. Good reports. Just beyond the parish albergue on the other side of the road.

Albergue La Encina **PR** (16) avda/Suero de Quiñones - ♥ 10€. ♥️ 8-10€. Bft 3-4.50€. **K W D @.** Cold drinks. Bike storage. 3 rooms - ♥ ♥ 38€. ☎ 987 361 087.

Albergue Verde **PR** (26÷2) avda/Fueros de León - ♥9€. ♥️ & bft - donativo (vegetarian-organic produce from own garden). **W D.** Yoga/meditation. **X Jan & Feb.** ☎ 689 927 926.

Camino Francés 2018/19

H *Hostal Suero de Quiñones,* on the route, 9 rooms - 👤 45€. 👤 👤 65€. ☎ 987 388 238. www.donsuero.es. | *Hostal Rural Nuestro Señora de Lourdes* c/Sierra Pambley. 9 rooms - 👤 30€. 👤 👤 45€, B&B. 🍽. **X Christmas.** ☎ 987 388 253 www.nuestrasenoradelourdes.es. | *El Caminero* c/Sierra Pambley. 4 rooms - 👤 35€. 👤 👤 40-60€. Bft 5-10€. 🍽 25€. ☎ 987 389 020. www.elcaminero.es.

⇨ There is a choice of two routes to Astorga. Again both are waymarked. The traditional way via the road route is tedious. The modern alternative, the walkers' route on quiet minor roads and tracks, is much more attractive and safer. The two routes meet at San Justo de la Vega.

Road route to Astorga (15 km)

⇨ At the end of town, keep straight on, follow disused road initially. On reaching the main road, turn right and continue on this road for about 12 km.

12 km to San Justo de la Vega 269

H *Hostal Juli* 8 rooms - 👤 20-30€. 👤 👤 35-40€, bft incl. 🍽 8-12€. ☎ 987 617 632.

Walkers route to Astorga (17 km)

⇨ At the end of town, at a yellow arrow on the next to last house, turn right. The route follows a marked track. Unsuitable for touring bikes when wet.

2 km to Villares de Orbigo 281

A *Albergue Villares de Orbigo* **PR** (24) - 👤 7€. 🍽 & bft donativo. Good showers and toilets. **W @.** 2 rooms - 👤 👤 30-40€. Open 11.00-23.00. **X Dec-Jan**. Call out of season. ☎ 987 132 935. A large ochre coloured house opposite the village bar.

Albergue El Encanto **PR** (10 + 6 rooms) Camino Santiago 23. 👤 14€ (inc bkfst). 👤 👤 50€. 👤 👤 👤 70€. **WD @.** ☎ 987 388 126, 682 860 210. albergueelencanto.es

Small grocery shop, open 10.00-14.00 and 16.00-21.00 Mon-Sat. Medical centre open Mon, Wed and Fri. Pharmacy open 10.00-14.00 and 17.00-20.00 on weekdays. The bar opposite the albergue serves food in the evening, except on Sundays.

3 km to Santibañez de Valdeiglesia 278

A *Parochial Albergue de Santibanez* (20÷4) - ⭧ 5€. 🍽 & bft donativo. **X Nov-Feb.** ☎ 987 377 698. Key from Sra Dominguez, no 5 in same street. One bar - drinks, snacks, bocadillos.

Albergue Camino Francés c/Real 68 **PR** (14) - ⭧ 7€. **W D B @.** ☎ 987 361 014. alberguecaminofrances@gmail.com

9 km to San Justo de la Vega

H *Hostal Juli* 8 rooms - ⭧ 20-30€. ⭧ ⭧ 35-40€, bft incl. 🍽 8-12€. ☎ 987 617 632.

3 km to Astorga (pop 13,802 alt 869 m) via the Roman bridge 266

A small, attractive city with important and extensive Roman remains, including substantial sections of its Roman walls (guided tours daily). The Cathedral is 15th/17th c. and has a fine portico. The figure on top of the pinnacle of the tower is that of *maragato* who, legend has it, fought at the battle of Clavijo. The interesting Diocesan museum (10.00-14.00 & 16.00-20.00) with 12th c. tomb paintings is attached to the Cathedral. The most striking building in the city is the *Palacio Episcopal*, known to one and all as the *Gaudí* building after its architect. It is in great contrast with the Cathedral only a few metres away. It contains the *Museo de los Caminos*, a collection of pilgrimage artifacts. Open in the summer daily 10.00-14.00 & 16.00-20.00, and in the winter Mon-Sat 11.00-14.00 & 15.30-18.30. 2€ or 4.50€ for a joint ticket to this and the Diocesan museum. In the 18-19th c. Astorga was the chocolate centre of Spain. Today almost all that is left is the *Museo del Chocolate*, c/José María Goy. Mon-Sat 12.00-14.00 & 18.00-20.00, Sun 12.00-14.00. Roman remains have been found near the Church of San Francisco. There is also a new Roman museum, entry 1.50€. The *Ayuntamiento* is 17th c with figures in traditional *maragato* dress that chime the hours on the clock.

Gaudi's Palacio Episcopal, Astorga

Church and Mass - Mass available in the Cathedral and in a number of other churches in Astorga. The Fransiscans in the Convento Sancti Spiritus have a daily evening Mass at 19.00. The Redemptorists church in the Calle Padres Redentoristas has pilgrim vepsers in the summer months.

⇨ *On Tuesday there is a large open-air market in Astorga. The centre is crowded and yellow arrows may be obscured.*

A *Albergue Camino y Vía* **PR** (22) ctra/León 64 - ✝ 7€. Bft 2€. Open all day. **X Nov-Feb.** Laundry, heating. ☎ 987 615 192. On main road into Astorga.

Albergue Público Siérvas de María (155) pl/San Francisco 3 - ✝ 5€. **K W D @**. **Open all year.** 11.00-22.00. Leave 06.00-08.00. ☎ 987 616 034. At the start of the town.

⇨ *Situated behind the Ayuntamiento and just past the old municipal albergue, which is now rarely used. If lost, ask for the Jardín de la Sinagoga.*

Albergue de Peregrinos San Javier **PR** (95) c/Portería 6 - ♀ 9€. Bft 4€. **K @.** Bike storage. **Open all Year.** 08.30-22.30. ☎ 987 618 532. Close to the Cathedral.

H *Hotel Gaudí,* very central location, near Cathedral - ♀ ♀ 60+€. Good restaurant. Pilgrim *menú* 12€, on production of *credencial.* ☎ 987 615 654. www.gaudihotel.es

La Peseta Hotel & Restaurante Plaza de San Bartolomé (nr *Ayuntamiento*) - ♀ 50€. Well known restaurant. ☎ 987 617 275. www.restaurantelapeseta. com. | *Pensión García* c/Bajada Postigo 3 - ♀ 30€. ☎ 987 616 046. Near the *Ayuntamiento.* A traditional pilgrim stop. Rte closed Sunday evening. | *Hotel Restaurante Astur Plaza**** Plaza de España 2 - ♀ ♀ 55€. ☎ 987 617 665.

www.hotelasturplaza.es | *Hostal Restaurante Coruña* Avda/Ponferrada 72 - ♀ ♀ 55€. ♀ ♀ ♀ 70€. ☎ 987 615 009. www.hostalcoruna.net.

ⓘ Plaza Eduardo Castro, 5. Next to Hotel Gaudí. ☎ 987 618 222. 10.00-13.30 & 16.00-19.00. Very helpful staff. **X Sunday pm and Monday.**

As you leave Astorga you are heading into the mountains. The stretch between Astorga and Ponferrada is one of the most interesting and beautiful of the whole Camino. *As far as the* Cruz de Ferro *you pass through the* Maragatería. *The inhabitants of Astorga and 45 villages to the west and south are known as* maragatos. *Their ethnic origins are unknown for certain, perhaps the Phoenicians, perhaps the Berbers in the 9th c. Whichever, they were a race apart and for centuries were the muleteers of Spain, doing the job now done by 38 tonne trucks. A proud people who are renowned for their honesty and with unique customs.*

WARNING: *It is a long and hard 50+ km across the mountains of León from Astorga to Ponferrada. The route goes up to 1500 m and, as in all mountains, the weather can change without warning. Take warm clothes and waterproofs, even in summer. Basic food can be bought along the way (there is a food shop in Rabanal in summer) and there are bars (with meals) in all inhabited villages. The route is uphill virtually all the way for over 30 km; and steeply downhill thereafter.*

⇨ *Leaving Astorga the route is now well waymarked.*

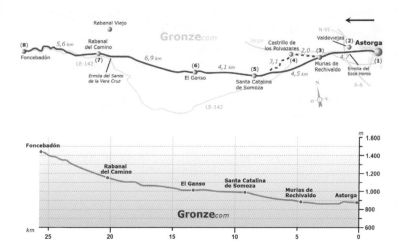

1 km to Valdeviejas 265

A *Albergue Municipal Ecce Homo* (10÷4) Antiguas Escuelas, about 100 m off the route to the right, signed - **⋔ 5€**. **W,** coins in slot. Drying space behind the albergue. **K.** The *Centro Social* is in the adjacent building, where vending machines offer a range of food and drink. **X Dec-Feb.**

4 km to Murias de Rechivaldo 261

A *Albergue Municipal* (20÷1) - **⋔ 5€**. No heating. **Open all Year**. Open all day to 22.30. Key from House no 17, on left when entering village on the camino but on LH side of the road that runs through the village.

Albergue las Aguedas **PR** (40÷2) c/Camino de Santiago 52 - **⋔ 9€** (+ 3€ for heating in winter). **⋔⊙⋔ 10€**. Bft 3.50€. Also 5 rooms - **⋔ ⋔ 45-50€**, including bft. **X Dec-Feb. ☎** 636 067 840.

A&H *Hosteria Casa Flor* **PR** (10) carretera Santa Columba - **⋔ 10€**. **⋔⊙⋔ 10€**. Bft 3€. **@.** Also 8 rooms - **⋔ ⋔ 49€**. **X Christmas. ☎** 987 603 148.

H *Casa rural La Veleta* Plaza Mayor. 7 rooms - **⋔ 40€**. **⋔ ⋔ 55€**, bft included. **⋔⊙⋔ 10€. ☎** 616 598 133. If you do not speak Spanish call **☎** 639 099 659.

Mesón El Llar - on the left as you walk through the village, friendly and good food.

☞ **Detour:** From Murias it is possible to divert to Castrillo de los Polvazares, a totally restored *Maragato* village. Now a national monument and a regular tourist stop.

⇨ **To get there turn left on to the tarmac road outside the municipal albergue. This takes you directly to Castrillo. It will add perhaps 1 km to your journey.**

A *Albergue Municipal* (8) c/Jardín - ♦ 5€. **X Nov-Mar.** ☎ 655 803 706.

H *Hostería Cuca la Vaina* 7 rooms - ♦ 45€, ♦ 60€, including bft. ♦ 16-17€. **X Monday** (except restaurant). ☎ 987 691 034. South of church. www.cucalavaina.es. | *Hostal/Restaurante Casa Coscolo* c/La Magdalena 1 - ♦ 40€. ♦ 50€. ☎ 987 691 984. www.casacoscolo.com

Mesón del Arriero on Rt as you enter village. Lunch from 14.00 consists of a *cocido maragato*, the regional speciality. About 12€ for the full meal, but two can share. Likewise at *Mesón La Magdalena*, further into the village, from 14.30.

⇨ To rejoin the Camino walk through the village until near the far side, bear left at a fork and follow yellow arrows uphill on a track.

5 km to Santa Catalina de Somoza (alt 997 m) 256

A *Albergue-Hostal-Hospedería San Blas* **PR** (20÷2) - ♦ 5€. ♦ 8.50-14€. Bft 4€. Eight rooms - ♦ 30€. ♦ 35-40€. **Open all year**. Albergue open 13.00-22.30. Bar from 06.00 (08.00 in winter). On left side of the road through the village just after the church.

Albergue-Hostal El Caminante **PR** (20÷2) - ♦ 5€ (+3€ in winter for heating). ♦ 9-14€. Bft 2-4€. Plus 12 rooms - ♦ 20€. ♦ 35-45€. **X Christmas.**

Pilgrim souvenirs, Santa Catalina de Somoza

4.5 km to El Ganso 251

A *Albergue Gabino* **PR** (31÷3) - ⍭ 8€. **K W D. X Dec-Feb.** ☎ 660 912 823. On the right at the end of the village.

H. *Bar Merendero La Barraca* - ⍁ 8-10€. Open from 07.30. **X Nov-Apr**.

⇨ Beware of *Ruta de Oro* signs hereabouts and do NOT turn right to Rabanal Viejo (at a Y junction 4 km after El Ganso).

7 km to Rabanal del Camino (pop 50 alt 1149 m) 244

In the 12th c. a hermit named Gaucelmo (hence the name of the albergue in Rabanal) obtained permission from the King to build a church and a hospice for pilgrims in *Foncebadón*, the next village on the Camino. The original document giving permission is in the Diocesan Museum in Astorga and you can see a copy in the entrance hall of the *Refugio Gaucelmo*. The ruined buildings outside the village on the left of the camino as you leave Foncebadón are the remains of the church and hospice built by Gaucelmo.

Church and Mass - *Benedictine monastery of San Salvador de Monte Irago. The monks welcome pilgrims who wish a spiritual retreat for a minimum 3 nights which must be arranged in advance.* ☎ *987 631 528. Pilgrims wishing to speak to the monks may do so between 17.00 and 18.45.* **Vespers at 19.00, Compline at 21.00, with pilgrim blessing and blessing of stones traditionally left at the Cruz de Ferro. Lauds at 07.30 and Mass at 12.30. All pilgrims are invited.**

A *Albergue Gaucelmo* (40÷3) opposite Santa María - *Donativo.* Afternoon tea and bft provided. **K.** Clothes washing and outdoor drying facilities. Opening time depends on hospitaleros' work requirements. Doors locked 22.30. Leave before 08.00. **X Nov-Mar.** ☎ 987 631 647 No reservations and preference given to walkers. No groups or people with any back-up transport, including of rucksacks. The albergue is the former presbytery, converted by the Confraternity of Saint James, in collaboration with the El Bierzo branch of Los Amigos in Ponferrada in 1991.

Refugio Gaucelmo, Rabanal del Camino

Albergue-Bar Nuestra Señora del Pilar **PR** (72÷2) - ⑂ 5€. ⑩ 8€. Bft 3€. **K.** 4 rooms - 35€. Accepts groups. Albergue **open all year** and all day until 23.00. Bar closed in low season. ☎ 987 631 621.

Albergue de la Junta Vecinal (32÷2) pl/Jeronimo - 🚹 5€. **K.** Wood burning stove. Open 12.00-22.00. **X Nov-Feb**.

Albergue La Senda **PR** (34÷4) - 🚹 5-7€. **K W D**. Open 10.00-22.00. **X Nov-Feb**. Campsites. ☎ 669 167 038. At the entry to the village.

H *Hostería el Refugio* c/Real 16 rooms - 🚹 35-50€. 🚹 🚹 50-60€. 🍽 11-20€. Bft 5€. ☎ 987 631 592. Run as a unit with *Bar Mesón El Refugio* by Antonio Pérez and his family. Very pilgrim friendly. Good food. Lunch 13.30-15.30. Dinner from 19.00 (reserve). *Menú* 11€. Bft 07.00. *Sello.* ☎ 987 631 592. On the camino beside Santa María. www.hostalelrefugio.es | *Hostal-Restaurante La Posada de Gaspar* c/Real 27. 11 rooms - 🚹 41-68€. 🚹 🚹 54-68€. 🍽 11€. Bft (from 07.00) 7€. Reserve ☎ 987 691 079. www.laposadadegaspar.com. | *Posada El Tesín* 4 rooms - 🚹 36€. 🚹 🚹 43€. Bar and restaurant. 🍽 10€. Bft 2.60-7€. ☎ 652 277 268. On camino as you enter village. www.posadaeltesin.com. | *The Stone Boat* B&B Calle Real 7 ☎ 652660504 hola@stoneboat.com

2 small shops near Gaucelmo refuge - one open all year, the other closed from late September to mid/late April.

☞ The *Ermita del Bendito Cristo de la Vera Cruz* on the left as you approach the village. Immediately after the Ermita the Camino bears right up the c/Real, whilst the modern tarmac road goes on up to the village square. Further up you pass the site of the original pilgrim hospital (now a private house with a ramp outside) and the 18th c. Church of *San José,* before reaching the Romanesque Church of *Santa María.*

Camino out of Rabanal

6 km to Foncebadón (alt 1495 m) 238

A *Domus Dei de Foncebadón* (18÷1) - *Donativo*. Bed, supper and bft. Open all Day. **X Nov-Mar**. In part of the church. Basic, but very popular. Volunteer wardens. Evening Prayer after dinner.

Albergue de Monte Irago **PR** (34÷2) - 🛏 5€. 🍽 9€. Bft 3.50€. **K W D. Open all year.** ☎ 695 452 950. Friendly, food is hearty and plentiful. On left on entering the village.

Albergue La Cruz de Ferro **PR** (34÷2) - 🛏 10€. Bft 3€. **W D. Open all year**.

La Posada del Druida **PR** (20) c/Real - 🛏 7. **W D.** ☎ 696 820 136. laposadadeldruida@gmail.com

A&H *Albergue/Hotel/Restaurant* - *El Convento de Foncebadón* (30÷3) - 🛏 7€. 🍽 10€. Bft 3€. Dormitories with no windows. Also 12 rooms - 🛏 36€. 🛏 50€. **X Jan-Feb.** ☎ 658 974 818 | **A & H** *Al Trasgu* **PR** c/Real - 🛏 24€. 🛏 🛏 36€. ☎ 987 053 877. www.eltrasgudefoncebad.wixsite.com/eltrasgu

H *Restaurante-Bar La Taberna de Gaia*. 12.00-20.00, May-November.

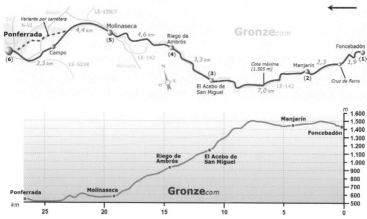

2 km to Cruz de Ferro (1505 m) A famous landmark on the camino, originally to help pilgrims find their way across the mountains. Nowadays each pilgrim may add a stone, brought from home, to the huge cairn below the cross. The Santiago chapel built from the stone of the ruined Church of San Roque in Manjarín, dates from Holy Year 1982.

Camino Francés 2018/19

Cruz de Ferro

2 km to Manjarín (1451 m) 234

A *Refugio de los Templarios.* An abandoned village except for this simple and very basic albergue run by Tomás Martínez de Paz, who devotes his life year round to caring for pilgrims. Mattresses for 20. Basic w.c. Outdoor kitchen. No heating, no showers. Evening meal. Open all year. *Donativo.*

Soon after Manjarín, at an obvious summit on the road, just below a military radar station, you are at 1517 *m - the highest point on the whole* Camino Francés.

7 km to El Acebo (1145 m) 227

Village giving a glimpse of a now almost vanished world. The houses are very old but are still inhabited. Balconies overhang the road. There is a central gutter in the road and cows wander about in the village. The church has a statue of *Santiago Peregrino.*

Church and Mass - *Iglesia de San Miguel Arcángel.* **Mass Tues, Thurs, Friday at 19.00 – confirm at the Albergue Parroquial.**

A *Albergue Mesón El Acebo* **PR** (18÷1) - ♦ 7€. ▒ 10-15€. Bft 4.50€, served from 07.00. Also 2 rooms - ♦ ♦ 22€. Open 07.00-20.00. **X Dec-Jan.** ☎ 987 695 074. Modern but cramped and no heating. 7 bunks in the Mesón itself, and 10 places in 2 other sites.

Parrochial Albergue (20÷1) - *Donativo*. **K @.** Some heating. Communal dinner. Bft offered. Volunteer Hospitaleros/as. Good reports. Near the church. Bar/shop nearby.

Albergue La Casa del Peregrino **PR** (96÷7) - ♀ 8-10€. ◉ 10€. Bft 3-5€. Swimming pool. Also 3 rooms - ♀ 35€. ♀ ♀ 50€. Open 11.00-23.00. **X Dec-Jan.** ☎ 987 057 875.

H *Casa Rural La Casa del Peregrino* c/Real 67-69. 4 rooms - ♀ 35€. ♀ ♀ 50€, including bft. ◉ 12€. Bike storage. ☎ 987 057 875. Under the same management as the Albergue above. www.lacasadelperegrino.es. | *Casa Rural La Trucha*, half way down on the left, 3 rooms - ♀ ♀ 45€, bft included. ◉ 10€ (vegetarian/organic). Good reports, **Open all year**. www.casarural-elaceho.com. | *Casa de Monte Irago*. Small and simple, 3 rooms - ♀ 20€. ♀ ♀ 40€ double. ◉10€. ☎ 653 842 263. | *Casa Rural La Rosa del Agua* - ♀ 35€. ♀ ♀ 50€. ☎ **616 849 738.** www.larosadelagua.com

4 km to Riego de Ambrós (920 m)

A *Albergue Santa Maria Magdalena* (30÷2) - ♀ 6€. **K.** Open 12.30-22.30. **X Nov-Feb.** By the side of Ermita de San Sebastián.

H *Mesón Ruta Santiago*. Rooms - ♀ 12€. ♀ ♀ 24€. ◉ 7€. **Open all year**. ☎ 987 695 190. Up by the main road. | *Pension Riego de Ambrós* ctra/de Astorga, 3. Four rooms - ♀ 20-25€. ♀ ♀ 35-40€. Bft 3€. **K.** ☎ 987 695 188.

2 other bars, both friendly.

⇨ *Note for walkers: the path from Riego to Molinaseca involves some steep descents. Take care.*

Roman Bridge over Río Maruelo

Camino Francés 2018/19

4.5 km to Molinaseca (pop 744 alt 585 m) 218

A *Albergue Municipal San Roque* (30÷1) - ♦ 6€. **W D**. Cooker, sink. **Open all year.** Tents with mattresses and bunks on veranda for summer overflow. Priority to walkers. Cyclists may have to wait until after 20.00. If closed, obtain the key from Alfredo, who lives next to *Bodega la Rana* (closed) near *Supermercado Elias.* ☎ 615 302 390. A chalet-style converted church, 500 m after turning onto the Ponferrada road at the western edge of the village.

Albergue Santa Marina **PR** (38) - ♦ 7€. ◉ 8€. Bft 3€. **NK.** Comfortable beds in large airy rooms. About 50 m before the municipal albergue. ☎ 987 453 077.

Albergue Compostela **PR** (30) c/Iglesia 39 - ♦ 9€. **X Nov-Mar.** ☎ 987 453 057.

H *Hostal El Horno* c/Rañadero 3 - ♦ 42€. ♦ 50€. ☎ 987 453 203. www. hostalelhorno.com. | *Hotel Rst El Palacio* Calle del Palacio - ♦ 50€. ☎ 987 453 094. www.casaelpalacio.com. | *The Way Hostel and Suites* c/el Palacio 10 - ♦ 42€. ♦ 50€. ♦ ♦ 65€. English spoken ☎ 637 941 017. www.facebook. com/thewayhostelmolinaseca. | *El Caprichio de Josana* Plaza del Santo Cristo - ♦ 43€. ♦ ♦ 60€. ☎ 987 453 167/644 448 204. | *Casa Rural Pajarapinta* c/Real 30 - ♦ 35€. ♦ ♦ 50€. ☎ 987 453 040. www.casaruralpajarapinta.es. | *Hostal De Floriana* - ♦ 55€. ♦ ♦ 65€. ☎ 987 453 146. www.defloriana.com. | *Hostal El Reloj* - ♦ ♦ 40€. ☎ 987 453 124. www.molinaseca.com

An attractive small town you enter over the Romanesque *Puente de Peregrinos.* Below it the river is dammed in the summer to provide excellent swimming. Two shops, including a *Supermercado* which may not stick to advertised hours (but you are only 8 km from Ponferrada). *Farmacia* on main road 800 m before the albergues.

8 km to Ponferrada (pop 66.027 alt 543 m) 210

A city in two distinct halves: the unspoilt and picturesque old quarter and, across the river Sil, the modern and commercial area. The imposing 12th c. *Castillo de los Templarios* is everyone's idea of a medieval Templar castle. Admission 6€. Other museums of interest in the Casco Viejo are Museum del Bierzo and the Radio Museum. Further out from the centre is the Energy Museum. All museums are closed on Mondays and are free on Wednesdays. The *Plaza del Ayuntamiento* has an impressive 17th c. City Hall. The Church of *Nuestra Señora de la Encina* (holm oak) is also worth seeing. The Chapel of the *Convento de la Purísima Concepción*, located on the Calle del Reloj on the left of the street leading to the *Plaza Mayor,* has a beautiful ceiling.

Castillo de los Templarios, Ponferrada

Church and Mass - *Basílica de Nuestra Señora de la Encina.* **Mass daily at 11.00 & 20.00.** *Iglesia de San Pedro -* **Mass daily 20.00.**

For other churches and Mass times: ⓘ Tourist Office is at c/Gil y Carrasco 4, open Mon-Sat 10.00-14.00 & 16:30-19:30 (hours vary seasonally).

A *Albergue San Nicolás de Flüe* (200) c/de la Loma - *Donativo.* All facilities. Accommodation in rooms with four bunks, large dormitories in the basement. Pilgrim Open hours vary seasonally. 13:00 in summer. Chapel of Nuestra Señora del Carmen is in the grounds. Colorful ceiling frescos depict the camino. Mass at 20:00 on Sundays.

Albergue Alea **PR** (18) c/Teleno 33 - ✝ 10€. **W D@.** ☎ 987 404 133. www.alberguealea.com

Albergue Guiana **PR** (90) c/del Castillo 112 - ✝ 12. **M W D @.** ☎ 987 409 327. info@albergueguiana.com

Camino Francés 2018/19

H There is a good selection of hostel and hotel accommodation in Ponferrada. This is a small selection. In the centre just under the Clock Tower, is the *Hotel Los Templarios* c/Flores Osorio 3 - ♦ 35€. ♦ 45€. Menu del dia 10€. ☎ 987 411 484. www.hotellostemplarios.es. | *Hotel Aroi Bierzo* Plaza del Ayuntamiento - ♦ 55€. ♦ ♦ 60€. ☎ 987 409 001. www.aroihoteles.com

Mainly in the modern quarter over the bridges (the 11th c iron bridge, since modernised, gave the city its name): *Hostal San Miguel*, Opp Mercado de Abastos - ♦ 25€. ♦ 36€. ☎ 987 426 700. www.hostalsanmiguelponferrada. es. | *Hostal Río Selmo* c/Río Selmo 22 - ♦ 35€. ♦ ♦ 50€ ☎ 987 402 665. www. hostalrioselmo.com

Possible excursion in Ponferrada: Santo Tomás de las Ollas is a delightful 10th c. Mozarabic church with Moorish horseshoe arches and Visigothic elements, in a village on the eastern side of the city. Go up the main NVI, here called the Avda de Astorga, and turn up by Hospital Camino de Santiago. Not a long walk. If closed, ask at number 7 on the right for the key.

⇨ *The route out of Ponferrada: start in the Plaza del Ayuntamiento where a smart embossed* concha *on a newsvendor's kiosk indicates the descending road down to the bridge across the river where waymarks, blue panels with yellow arrows indicating the route, are attached to street lights and other street furniture. You will find the first panel attached to a post indicating a turn to the right almost immediately after crossing the bridge. You may walk through town, or take a pleasant stroll along the River Sil through Concordia Park.*

☞ *In the barrio of Compostilla look out for friezes on the wall of a church, and in Columbrianos. Also here Bar Moderno.*

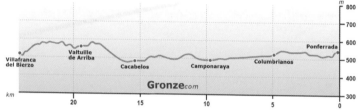

(*) Distancia de Pieros a Villafranca por carretera

5 km to Columbrianos

A *Albergue San Blas* **PR** (20÷3) c/San Blas 5 - � 10€. |◉| **M W D @.** ☎ 675 651 241, 611 614 149 reservas@alberguesanblas.es www.alberguesanblas.es

H *Hotel Novo* (1 km before Columbrianos) - � 30€+. �pair 35€+. ☎ 987 424 441. www.hotelnovo.com

Casa Rural el Almendro de Maria c/Real 56 - � 65€. ☎ 633 481 100. www.elalmendrodemaria.com

2.5 km to Fuentes Nuevas 203

H *Bar La Ermita*. Pilgrims' book. *Taberno Mateo; La Casona.*

2 km to Camponaraya 201

A *Albergue La Medina* **PR** (20) c/Camino de Santiago 87 - ♺ 10€. **M W D @. Open all year.** ☎ 987 463 962.

Albergue Nayara **PR** (26) avda/de Galicia 506 - ♺ 8€. **@. X Oct-Mar.** ☎ 987 459 159. www.alberguenaraya.es

Camino Francés 2018/19

H *Bar Brazal,* 40 m off road on R. *Hogar del Pensionista* is pilgrim friendly. *Bar Goya* in the main square: a good place to stop. *Casa Paz* has a good *Menú del día. Hostal Nuevo Lugar -* ☎ 987 450 011, and *Hostal Mafaval -* ☎ 987 450 112, are both on the main road to A Coruña, some distance from the centre.

☞ **Detour.** *The Monastery of Carracedo* at the small village Carracedo del Monasterio. A 4 km detour to this large, impressive Cistercian monastery, open 10.00-13.00 & 16.00-19.00 (not Mon). There is a map in the Main Square of Camponaraya. The route is well waymarked with arrows: from the square follow the carretera de Narayola (2 kms), cross Narayola, and 2 kms more through the Calle Real, after crossing under the Autovía del Nordeste A-6, you reach the monastery.

Albergue and Hostal Ubaldo Nieto de Alba c/**Plaza de la Roda 1, Carracedelo** - ♦ 8€. ☎ 608 888 211. www.alojamientoubaldonieto.com

Leaving the albergue, you take the road to Cacabelos, 3 kms and you reach Cacabelos center.

Cacabelos

5 km to Cacabelos (pop 4903 alt 486 m) 195

A town in the heart of the fruit and wine growing region of El Bierzo. Excellent wines, but hardly known outside Spain. The village has interesting buildings and a shop, built on the site of the former San Lázaro Hospital, one of five such hospitals in Cacabelos.

Church and Mass - *Iglesia de Santa María de la Plaza.* **Mass daily at 19.00.**

A *Albergue Municipal* (70÷35) - ⍭ 6€. **W D.** Open 14.00-23.00. Leave 08.00. **X Nov-Apr.** ☎ 987 547 167. On the right soon after the bridge over the Rio Cua on the way out of town.

Albergue-Hostal La Gallega (30) c/Santa María - ⍭ 10€. ⍩ 10€. Bft 4.50€. Dinner. Plus 19 rooms - ⍭ 25€. ⍭ ⍭ 40€. Open 11.00-23.00. **X Feb.** ☎ 987 549 476.

Bar Pensión El Molino has bunks at 10€ & rooms from 22€. ⍩ 6-10€. The owner speaks good English.

H *Hostal Santa María* - 30-45€. ☎ 987 549 588. www.hostalsantamaria.net. | *Bar/ Café Gallega* has rooms ⍭ 25€| ⍭ ⍭ 40€. *2nd* floor better, as bar can be noisy. ☎ 987 549 476. | Hotel Moncloa de San Lazaro c/Cimadevilla 97 - ⍭ 50€, with breakfast. Shop, restaurant, bar. ☎ 987 546 101. www.moncloadesanlazaro.com

Méson El Apóstol Santa María 27, half way on route through town, before market and church. Good 9€ *menú*. *Méson El Refugio de Saul,* c/Calexa Sixtina. Good 8€ *menú*.

2 km to Pieros

A *Albergue Pieros El Serbal y La Luna* **PR** (18) c/El Pozo 15 - ⍭ 5€. ⍩ 9€. Bft 3€. Dinner 9€ **W D. X Dec-Feb.** ☎ 639 888 924.

Shortly after passing through the village of Pieros, a well-marked turn to the right offers a very pleasant route through vineyards and away from the highway. It passes through the village of Valtuille de Arriba, where there is a small *Casa Rural*: *La Osa Mayor,* c/El Besal. 5 rooms - 30€ B&B. **Open all year.** ☎ 987 562 185.

5 km to Villafranca del Bierzo

Popular stopping point for pilgrims before tackling the climb into the mountains and Galicia. Pilgrims arrive almost immediately at the Romanesque Church of *Santiago* with its *Puerta del Perdón.* Pilgrims who made it this far but were too sick or injured to continue to Santiago were, once they had crossed through the 'door of forgiveness', granted all the same benefits and indulgences as if they had completed their pilgrimage. The Church of *San Francisco* has a *mudéjar* ceiling. If locked keys for both churches are held by the bookshop in the main square.

Church and Mass - *Colegiata de Santa María.* **Mass daily 19.00.** *Convento de la Concepción (Padres Paúles) -* **Mass daily 08.30.** *Convento de San José -* **Mass daily 20.00.** For more information on Mass times: ⓘIn Alameda Alta, past the Church of San Nicolás (summer only).

A *Municipal Albergue* (60÷5) - ⚲ 6€. **K @.** Bike storage. Open 12.00-22.00. **X Dec-Feb.** ☎ 987 542 356. The first building on the right on entering the town, 150 metres before the Santiago church.

Albergue Ave Fenix (77) - ⚲ 5€. ⓘ 7-8€. Bft 3€. **NK.** Near the church of Santiago. **Open all year.** ☎ 987 540 229. albergueavefenix@gmail.com. www.albergueavefenix.com

Albergue de la Piedra **PR** (26÷2) Espíritu Santo 14 - ⚲ 8€. Bft 2€. **K.** Also 6 rooms - ⚲ 20-24€. ☎ 987 540 260. Over the bridge out of town on the route to Pereje.

Albergue Leo **PR** (24) c/Ribadeo 10 - ⚲ 10€. Each bunk has own light & plug. **W D K @.** Bike storage. Open 12.00-22.30. **X Dec-Feb.** ☎ 987 542 658/658 049 244. www.albergueleo.com

Villafranca del Bierzo

Hospedería San Nicolás el Real (30÷3) trav/Nicolás - ♦ 5€. ♦️ 12€. ☎ 987 540 483.

Albergue El Castillo **PR** (24) c/Castillo 8 - ♦ 10€. **X Nov-Mar.** ☎ 987 540 344. www.alberguelcastillo.es

Albergue La Yedra (18) c/La Yedra 9 - ♦ 10€. **W D K @.** ☎ 636 586 872. alberguelayedra@gmail.com

H *Hostal Comercio*, Puente Nuevo - ♦ from 15€. ☎ 987 540 008. | *Hotel San Francisco* Plaza Mayor 6 - ♦ 40€. ♦ 50€. ☎ 987 540 465. www. hotelsanfrancisco.org. | *Hotel El Cruce* San Salvador 37, 10 minutes walk from the centre, but welcoming - ♦ 18€. ♦ ♦ 25€. ♦ ♦ ♦ 33€. ☎ 987 540 185. http:// www.hostalcruce.es. | *Hostal Restaurante Mendez* c/Espíritu Santo 1 - ♦ 43€. ♦ ♦ 50€. ☎ 987 540 055. www.restaurantemendez.com. | *Apartamentos el Camino* Calle Salinas 7 1B - ♦ ♦ 50€, up to 4 people. Booking: www.a-hotel.com/ spain/villafranca-del-bierzo/1038992-apartamentos-el-camino/#apartments. | *Parador de Villafranca del Bierzo**** avda/Calvo Sotelo 28 - ☎ 987 540 175. www.parador.es/es/paradores/parador-de-villafranca-del-bierzo.

⇨ *It is a long hard climb from here to the mountain village of O Cebreiro in Galicia. Leaving Villafranca, walkers have two options: a largely road-based route; or a high level route (more strenuous, 2 km further, but quieter and beautiful). It is hard going whichever way you choose and less fit walkers may consider spending the night at Vega de Valcarce. Do not attempt the high level route in bad weather.*

Route 1. N6 route (27 km)

⇨ *When leaving Villafranca, cross the bridge and follow arrows to the left for 5 km. (Pereje, Albergue Municipal (30) single beds, kitchen, hot water, ☎ 699 512 004. The busy, friendly bar about 50 m away serves very good meals). Follow this road, and turn right at the N6 onto an obvious dedicated yellow painted footpath. The camino follows the N6 or, in places, the old N6. Completion of the new motorway to A Coruña has reduced the traffic using the N6 and new barriers at the roadside have improved safety, making this a much more pleasant walk. After a further 5 km, just after the marker for km 413, take a right turn onto the old N6 to Trabadelo.*

Route 2. High level route via Pradela (29 km)

⇨ *To the RH side of the N6 - starts as you cross the river bridge leaving Villafranca. Almost immediately after crossing you will find yellow arrows pointing between some buildings. Follow these arrows. They lead to a fairly good path which climbs gently initially but becomes quite steep in places. There is no need to enter Pradela. There is a bar here, Bar La Fócara, which may or may not be open. The route out is the tarmac road to Trabadelo, where you pick up Route 1. This route involves a steep climb, with beautiful views, and a steep descent. Avoid in bad weather.*

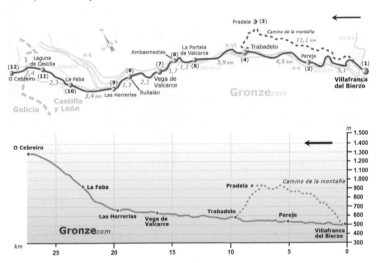

Route 1 to Trabadelo (12 km by Route 2)

⇨ *Turn left from Route 2 to go into the village.*

A *Albergue Municipal* (36÷6), at the far end of the village - ♦ 6€. **K.** Sandwiches. **X Nov-Mar.** ☎ 687 827 987.

Albergue Parroquial (22) c/La Iglesia. Reservations taken - ♦ 5€. **W D K. Open all year.** ☎ 630 628 130. www.albergueparroquialtrabadelo.com

Albergue Crispeta **PR** (48), at entrance to the village - ♦ 6-8€. 🍽 10€. Bft 4.50€. **W K.** Bar. ☎ 620 329 386.

Albergue Camino y Leyenda **PR** (16) c/Camino de Santiago - 🚹 10+€. **W D @.** ☎ 628 921 776. www.alberguecaminoyleyenda.com

Casa Susi, **PR** (12 single beds) - 🚹 5€. Breakfast and communal dinner for a donation. Organic vegetable garden, access to river, relaxing terrace. English spoken. **X Nov-Mar.** ☎ 683 278 778. www.facebook.com/alberguecasasusi

H *Hostal Nova Ruta.* 10 rooms - 🚹 25€. 🚹🚹 45€. 🍽 10€. Bft 4.50€. ☎ 987 566 431. www.hostalnovaruta.com. | *Bar Pension El Puente Peregrino.* 3 rooms - 🚹 30€. 🚹🚹 38€. 🍽 10€. Bft 2.50€. **X Dec-Feb.** ☎ 987 566 500. | *Casa Rural Os Arroxos*, on the route - 🚹 35€. 🚹🚹 40€. ☎ 987 566 529. www.osarroxos.es

⇨ **Turn right to continue on the old N6.**

On the way to La Portela de Valcarce

3.5 km to La Portela de Valcare

A *Albergue El Peregrino* **PR** (28) c/Camino de Santiago 5 - 🚹 10€. **Meals. @.** ☎ 987 543 197. www.laportela.com

H *Hotel-Restaurant-Tienda Valcarce.* 51 rooms - 🚹 30€. 🚹🚹 46-58€. ☎ 987 543 180. www.valcarcehoteles.com/hoteles/valcarce-camino-de-santiago

Camino Francés 2018/19

1.5 km to Ambas Mestas

A *Albergue de Peregrinos Das Animas* (14÷1) Campo Bajo 3**.** Bunk beds + 10 mattresses - ♦ 5€. Heating. **W. X Dec-Feb. ☎** 619 048 626. www.dasanimas.com

Albergue Camynos **PR** (10) Nacional VI Nº 43 - ♦ 10€. **Meals. W D @. ☎** 609 381 412. www.camynos.es

Albergue Casa Pescador **PR** (24÷3) ctra/Antigua N-VI - ♦ 10-12€ (has rooms). **W D K @. ☎** 603 515 868, 987 684 955. casitadelpescador@gmail.com. www. casadelpescador.eu

2.5 km to Vega de Valcarce (630 m) 170

A *Albergue Municipal* (64÷7), off plaza - ♦ 5€. **K W D. Open all year.** 13.00-21.00. Key from *Bar Charly*, whose food is good value and open for bft early (not Sun).

Albergue El Paso **PR** (28) Nacional N-VI Nº6 - ♦ 10€. **K W D @. Open all year. ☎** 628 104 309. www.albergueelpaso.es

Albergue El Rincón Apóstol **PR** (16) Nacional N-VI Nº1 - ♦ 17€ **B&B. W D @. ☎** 987 543 099.

Albergue Santa María Magdelena **PR** (15) Nacional N-VI - ♦ 9€. **K W D @. ☎** 987 543 230. alberguelamagdalena@yahoo.es

Albergue do Brasil – El Roble **PR** (18) ctra/Antigua N-VI. Donativo. **☎** 634 242 642

A&H *Pensión-Albergue Fernández* (16) - ♦ 8€. **K.** Also 9 rooms - ♦ 15€. ♦ 25-30€. **☎** 987 543 027.

2 km to Ruitelán 168

A *Albergue Pequeño Potala* **PR** (34÷3) - ♦ 5€. ♦ 8€. bft 3€. Communal meal. Bar selling foodstuffs and drinks. **☎** 987 561 322.

Albergue El Rincón de PIN **PR** (10÷1 + rooms) ctra/Antigua N-VI 41 - ♦ 10€. **W D @.** Communal Meal. **☎** 616 066 442. alberguepin@gmail.com

☞ Chapel dedicated to San Froilan, 10th c. bishop of León.

A *Albergue Las Herrerias* **PR** (12) - ⭧ 7€. Bft 3€. 🍽 Vegetarian from 8€. **X Nov-Feb.** ☎ 654 353 940.

Albergue Casa Lixa **PR** (30÷4 + rooms) Camino de Santiago 35. Meals **W D @.** ⭧ 11€. ☎ 987 134 915, 608 528 715. info@casalixa.com. www.casalixa.com

H. *Hotel Rural El Paraíso del Bierzo.* 13 rooms - ⭧ 38-44€. ⭧ ⭧ 49-59€. 🍽 13€. Bft 3.50-7€. **X Jan.** ☎ 987 684 137. On the main road. www.paraisodelbierzo. com. | *Pension-Restaurante A Casa do Ferreiro.* 8 rooms - ⭧ ⭧ 45€. 🍽 10€. Bft 3€, from 08.00. **X Nov-Mar weekdays**. ☎ 679 478 150. | *Pension-Restaurante-Casa Polín*. 4 rooms - ⭧ ⭧ 30-36€. 🍽 10€. Bft 3€. **Open all year**. ☎ 987 543 039. At the end of the village. www.casarestaurantepolin.es. | *Hostal Restaurante El Capricho de Josana*. 13 rooms - ⭧ 38-45€. ⭧ ⭧ 51-65€. Bft 7€. 🍽 10€. **X Feb.** Reservation required in low season. www.elcaprichodejosana.com

The village, mainly off road down in the river valley, has an English connection. The last houses in Herrerías were called *Hospital* in line with a Papal Bull of 1178 which mentioned a 'hospital of the English'. There was also a chapel where pilgrims who had died were buried.

There now follows a beautiful route up to O Cebreiro (only 8 km but very steep so allow adequate time), initially through chestnut woods and then through open country and a series of hamlets. There is a tarmac road to the first hamlet, La Faba, but walkers can turn left on a well signed track up through woods. Cyclists can continue, turning right at a junction, by-passing La Faba, and rejoining walkers at the second hamlet, Laguna de Castillo, but be warned it is a long climb. In bad weather, walkers are advised to take the cyclists' option. In atrocious weather, walkers are advised to take the slightly longer but safer tarmac road. The weather can be very bad here at any time of the year. Make sure that you have time to make it to O Cebreiro in daylight.

4 km to La Faba (alt 927 m)

A *German Association Albergue* (66÷3) - ⭧ 5€. Bft *donativo*. **K.** Open 14.00-22.00. Leave 08.30. **X Dec-Feb.**

Albergue El Refugio (8) - ⭧ 5€ (donation). Cafeteria, communal meal 10€. ☎ 654 911 223. caminarte.asociacion@gmail.com. www.caminarte.org

H. Bar-*El Ultimo Rincon del Bierzo* - 🍽 8.50 € (+ vegetarian menu), from 19.30. Bft 3€. Open Sundays.

Pilgrim statue at La Faba

Just before you reach O Cebreiro, you enter the fourth and last Autonomous Region traversed by the Camino Francés: Galicia (province of Lugo). Galicia has its own language, Gallego, and signs are often in this rather than Castilian.

The albergues in Galicia run by the Xunta of Galicia usually open at 16.00 or earlier, at 13.00, in high season. There is a local paid warden and whilst there may be a kitchen very few have a supply of pans. The standard charge is 6€. A disposable bed sheet and pillow case is provided. They may allow a second night stay, if space is available.

2 km to Laguna de Castilla (alt 1,175 m) (walkers)

A *Albergue A Escuela* **PR** (45), extension of the bar/rte of the same name - ♦ 10€. ⦿. **W D4€.** Also 2 rooms - ♦ ♦ 40€. Outside drying space. **X Nov-Feb.** ☎ 616 479 238.

2.5 km to O Cebreiro (pop 50 alt 1,300 m) 150

A tiny village of 20 houses which is a high point of the pilgrimage. Cebreiro developed from and for the pilgrimage. There was a hospital here from the 11th c. to 1854, run by monks from the 16th c. Abbey of St Gerard of Aurillac in France. The 12th c. Church of *Santa María* has relics including a 12th c. statue of the Virgin, which reputedly inclined its head after a miracle took place. Outside the church is a bronze bust of the late priest, D Elias Valiña, who devoted his life to O Cebreiro and to the practical and academic aspects of the pilgrimage. You can see pallozas nearby, the typical Galician thatched buildings of Celtic origin. In one is a small museum.

Souvenir shop, O Cebreiro

Church and Mass - *Iglesia Santa Maria A Real Do Cebreiro.* **Daily International Mass 19.00h, followed by pilgrim blessing.**

A *Albergue de la Xunta de Galicia* (104÷3) - 6€. **K,** with no utensils. Bike storage outside. **Open all year.** 13.00-22.00. Key from Hostal San Giraldo. Enquire at church in an emergency.

Albergue Casa Campela **PR** (10) - 🚹 12€. **W D @.** ☎ 679 678 458, 982 179 317. casacampelo@outlook.com

H *Hostal San Giraldo de Aurillac.* 6 rooms - 🚹 45€. 🚹 🚹 60€. Hotel 5 rooms - 🚹 40-45€. 🚹 🚹 50-60€. 🍽 10-13€. Bft 3.50€. **Open all year.** ☎ 982 367 182. www.hotelcebreiro.com. | *Hostal rural A Venta Celta.* 5 rooms - 🚹 🚹 40€. 🍽 10€. Bft 3€. **Open all year.** ☎ 667 003 556. | *Hostal-Restaurant Casa Anton*, on the road below the pallozas. 4 rooms - 🚹 🚹 40-45€, including bft. ☎ 982 151 336. | *Mesón Carolo.* 13 rooms - 🚹 40€. 🚹 🚹 48€. 🍽 10€. Bft 4€. **Open all year.** From 06.00 (in summer). ☎ 982 367 168.

Small shop selling basic supplies and several souvenir shops.

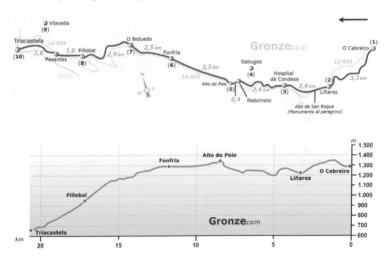

3 km to Linares (1,222 m)

A *Albergue Linar do Rei* **PR** (20) - 🚹 10€. **X Nov-Mar.** ☎ 616 464 831.

H *Casa Rural Jaime.* 4 rooms - 🚹 🚹 40€. 🍽 9€. Bft 3€. **X Nov-Epiphany.** ☎ 982 367 166.

Bar, shop and meals.

Look out for a dramatic modern bronze sculpture of a pilgrim at Alto San Roque between here and Hospital de la Condesa.

2.5 km to Hospital de la Condesa (alt 1241 m) 152

A *Albergue de la Xunta de Galicia* (20÷2) - 🚹 6€. **K,** without utensils. **W**. Open 13.00-22.00. **Open all year**.

H *Mesón O Tear*. 2 rooms - 🚹 🚹 30€. 🍽 10€. Bft. Open from 06.00 in high season and 08.30 in low season. **Open weekends only in low season**. ☎ 982 367 183.

3 km to Alto de Poio (or Porto de Poio) (1,337 m) 149

Albergue El Puerto **PR** (18) - 🚹 6€. Bar and restaurant. ☎ 982 367 172.

A&H Hostal/Rte *Santa María de Poio* **PR** (16÷2) - 🚹 9€. Plus 15 rooms - 🚹 30€. 🚹 🚹 40€. ☎ 982 367 167. Shop, *Café/Bar Puerto,* pilgrim book and *sello.*

3 km to Fonfría do Camino 146

A *Albergue A Reboleira-Centro de Turismo rural-Casa Nuñez* **PR** (80÷4) - 🚹 8€. Plus 8 rooms - 🚹 32€. 🚹 🚹 40€. 🍽 9€. Bft 3€. **X Nov-Feb.** ☎ 982 181 271.

H *Casa de Lucas* c/Fonfría 25 - 🚹 🚹 36€. ☎ 690 346 740. www.casadelucas.es. | *Casal Núñez* - 🚹 🚹 40€. ☎ 982 161 335. | *Casa Rural Galego* c/Fonfría 9 - 🚹 25€. 🚹 🚹 37€. ☎ 982 161 461.

2.5 km to Biduedo 143.5

Centro de Turismo Casa Quioga-Meson Betularia. 9 rooms - 🚹 🚹 35€. 🍽 10€. Bft 3.50-5€. Bocadillos and *sello.* ☎ 982 187 299.

2.5 km to Filloval 141

A *Albergue-Bar Tienda Aira do Camino* **PR** (18) - 🚹 10€. **K**. Two rooms - 🚹 🚹 30€. **X Dec-Jan.** ☎ 982 187 299.

4 km to Triacastela (alt 665 m) 137

Church and Mass - *Iglesia de Santiago, Plaza de la Iglesia.* Originally Romanesque, the church was rebuilt in the 18th c. **Mass at 18.00 daily.**

A *Albergue de la Xunta de Galicia* (56÷14) - 🚹 6€. **NK**. **Open all year.** 13.00-22.00. ☎ 660 396 811.

Albergue Aitzenea **PR** (38÷4) pl/Vista Alegre 1 - ♦ 8€. **K W D**3€. **X Nov-Mar.** ☎ 982 548 129.

Albergue Berceo do Camino **PR** (27) avda/Camilo José Cela 11 - ♦ 8€. **K W D. Open all year.** ☎ 982 548 127.

Refugio de Oribio **PR** (27÷2) avda/de Castillo 20 - ♦ 8-9€. **K @.** Good reports. Open all year and all day.

Centro de Turismo Rural Complexo Xacobeo (30) - ♦ 9€. ⦿ 10€. Bft 3-6€. **W**x2**D**x2 3€ **@.** Plus 6 rooms - ♦ ♦ 40€. **Open all day. X Christmas.** ☎ 982 548 037. Check in at *Bar Xacobeo* further down the street.

Albergue Atrio **PR** (20) c/Peregrino 1 - ♦ 9€. **K D W @.** ☎ 982 548 488.

Albergue Horta de Abel **PR** (14) c/Peregrino 5 - ♦ 9€. **K W D @.** ☎ 608 080 556.

Albergue Lemos **PR** (12) av/Castilla 24 - ♦ 9€. ♦ 35€. ♦ ♦ 40€. **K W D @. Open All Year.** ☎ 677 117 238.

H *Pensión-Restaurante-Bar Villasante* avda/Camilo José Cela 7. 10 rooms - ♦ 30€. ♦ ♦ 40€. ⦿ 10€. Bft 3-5€. **X Nov-Mar.** ☎ 982 548 116. | *Casa David.* 7 rooms - ♦ 35€. ♦ ♦ 50€. Bft 5€. **X Christmas.** ☎ 982 548 144. Off main road. | *Hospedaje O'Novo* avda/Camilo José Cela 14 - ♦ 20€. Bft 5€. ☎ 982 548 105. | *Hostal Pensión García* c/Peregrino 8 - ♦ 30€. ♦ ♦ 40€. ☎ 982 548 024. www. dormirentriacastela.com. | **A&H** *Casa Olga* Rúa do Castro -from 15€ per ♦. ☎ 982 548 134. www.hospedajecasaolga.com

Bar Río c/Leoncio Cadorniga 1. Welcoming, good meals. 10€ *menu.* Bocadillos and *Sello.* | *O Peregrino* bar, opposite the Xunta albergue, opens for breakfast at 07.30 and has a good *menú del día.*

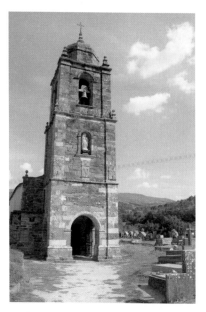

Church of Santiago, Triacastela

Church of Santiago - a very pilgrim friendly priest offers **Pilgrim Mass at 19.00 daily**.

2 *supermercados*, 2 banks and all facilities.

⇨ *There is a choice of two routes from Triacastela to Sarria. The first takes you through Samos with its famous monastery. The second, direct to Sarria and 3.5 km shorter, is the original camino - now partly tarmac. The Samos route, although longer, is very peaceful and shady and in true old camino style for long stretches.*

Camino Francés 2018/19

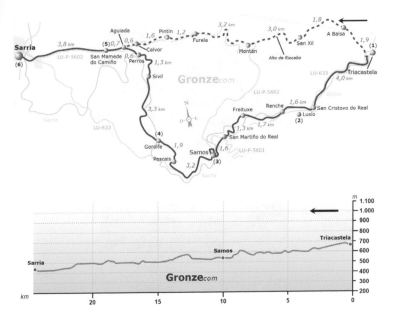

Sarria via Samos route (25 km)

⇨ *The L turn to San Cristobo and Samos at the western end of Triacastela is not well-waymarked.* Be aware that sometimes local businesses paint yellow arrows to divert pilgrims to their establishment. Yellow arrows may point you to the right to San Xil. To go to Samos, leave town and turn left onto LU633.

5 km to Lusio

⇨ Follow the pilgrim sign down to the right into San Cristobo off of LU633. If you stay on LU633 for 1km, you will arrive to *Albergue Casa Forte de Lusio* (60), which is open all year. The Albergue is fairly basic. There is a kitchen but it is not equipped with any utensils. You are now not too far from Samos where the accommodation options are better. If you don't intend to stay in Casa Forte de Lusio, be sure to take the right turn down into San Cristobo.

6 km to Samos

The path through San Cristobo (not on LU633) is on a forested trail most of the way to Samos, but with only a bar (may or may not be open) in Renche (1.7km after San Cristobo). After passing the tiny village of San Martino, you will see a sign welcoming you to Samos. The view gives you a perspective of the Monastery San Xulian.

Monasterio de Samos

Church and Mass - The history of the Benedictine monastery stretches back over the ages to the 11th c. and possibly earlier. The buildings show influences of the Gothic, Renaissance and Baroque styles. There are 30-minute tours between 09.30-12.30 & 16.30-18.30 for 4€. **Vespers 19.30 every day, followed by Mass.**

A *Monasterio San Julian y Santa Basilissa-Albergue-Hospedería* (70÷1) - *Donativo.* Hot showers, no heating. Hospedería - 15 rooms for those wishing to go on retreat **(3 days or longer) -** ✝ 35€ full board. **NK. Open all year.** 14.30-22.30. Leave 08.00. The entrance to the albergue is via a small door next to a petrol station built into the monastery walls. ☎ 982 546 046. www. abadiadesamos.com/hospederia.php

Albergue Val de Samos **PR** (48÷5) - ⚹ 9-11€. **K W**3€ **D**3€. Bike storage 1€. Stabling 8€. **X Dec-Feb**. In low season, groups only. Book in advance. ☎ 902 002 460/609 638 801. Overlooking the Monastery gardens.

Albergue Albaroque **PR** (10) c/Salvador 1 - ⚹ 9. **W D @. Open all year.**
☎ 982 546 087

A&H *Hostal Victoria* **PR** c/Salvador 4 - ⚹ 9€. ⚹ 25€. ⚹ 35€. ☎ 982 546 022.

H*CasaLicerio(CasaRural)*av/Compostela44.4rooms- ⚹ 30€. ⚹ 50.€ ⚹ ⚹ 60€. (Price inc laundry) ☎ 653 593 814. Email: casalicerio@gmail.com. Facebook, Instagram, Twitter @CasaLicerio. Across from *Supermercado Garza.* Under new management - owner is a native English speaker. | *Hotel-Restarante-Bar A Veiga* avda/Compostela 61. 15 rooms - ⚹ 24-35€. ⚹ 35-46€. 🍽 11€. Bft 5€, from 07.30. ☎ 982 546 052. On the road to Sarria after the village. www.hotelaveiga. com. | *Hostal-Restaurante-Bar-Albergue Victoria,* c/El Salvador 4 (8) - ⚹ 10€. 🍽 10€. Bft. Plus 8 rooms - ⚹ ⚹ 45€. **Albergue open all year.** From 06.00 (breakfast) in summer. www.hostal-victoria.es/es/index.php

Café Espana, plaza de España , has great cafés con leche and napolitanas. 2 *supermercados,* one at each end of the village. Better selection at the second one. Farmacia open Monday-Saturday.

Tourist Information office at the entrance to the Monastery albergue. Host has keys to the 9th c. chapel near the river on the north east side of town. Ask for entrance in the afternoon from 15.00 to 21.00.

15 km to Sarria (via Rio Oribio and avoiding most of the main road)**.** 2 km after leaving Samos, turn right at Restaurant Pontenovo to avoid walking on the road all the way to Sarria. Here you can enjoy the last truly peaceful part of the camino before the number of pilgrims significantly increases in Sarria. There are no services for the 7 km between Pontenovo and San Mamed, when the route connects with the San Xil route from Triacastela.

You pass the Romanesque cemetery Chapel of *Santa Eulalia de Pascais,* 12th c. shrine near **San Frollais** and the villages of **Fontan, Sivil, A Veiga, and Pieros** (Chapel of Virgen del Camino).

Direct route (18 km)

The old camino takes you through the villages of **A Balsa, San Xil, Furela and Calvor.**

Casa de Franco in Furela offers meals, snacks and has a small food shop. **Open all year.** From 08.30.

A Balsa *(2 km) Albergue El Beso* (12÷1) - 🚶 9€. 🍽 10€. Bft 4€. **Open all year**. An ecological albergue with a vegetarian dinner and breakfast offered. ☎ 633 550 558.

12 km to Pintin 126

H *Pensión-Restaurante-Bar Casa Cines*. 7 rooms - 🚶 35-45€. 🚶 🚶 35-60€. 🍽 10€. Bft 3€. ☎ 982 167 939. Will provide transport for those staying at Albergue Xunta de Calvor (below). Telephone booking needed.

2 km to Calvor 124

A *Albergue Xunta (22)* - 🚶 6€. **K,** with no utensils. Own food is recommended. See entry above for *Casa Cines* for transport for those wishing to dine there.

2 km to San Mamed 122

A *Albergue Paloma y Lena* **PR** (22÷3) - 🚶 10€. 🍽 9€ (vegetarian). Bft included. Plus 6 rooms - 🚶 30€. 🚶 🚶 40€. Booking necessary in low season. ☎ 982 533 248.

2.5 km to Sarria (pop 13000 alt 420 m) 120

Church and Mass - *Parroquia de Santa Marina.* **18.00 pilgrims' Mass.** *Convento de la Merced (Padres Mercedarios)* - **Mass 20.00 in summer.** *Iglesia de San Lázaro* - **Mass 19.00.**

Coat of Arms, Sarria

Remember – You can help the pilgrims who come after you

The guides published by the Confraternity of Saint James are written by pilgrims who have walked the routes. They are kept up to date with information sent by other pilgrims who use the guides. Please help your fellow pilgrims by keeping notes and reporting any changes to the route or to the accommodation listed. **Please email office@csj.org.uk with any suggestions.**

Note: from Sarria to Santiago the route gets a lot busier so you should plan carefully to secure your accommodation.

H **PR** *Vila de Sarria* - ♦ 7€. Cabin 25€. ☎ 982 535 467. **X Nov – Mar.** 1km
ore town.

Albergue de la Xunta de Galicia (35) r/Mayor 79 - ♦ 6€. **K,** no utensils. Bike
rage. **Open all year.** From 13.00. ☎ 660 396 813. Cross the river, turn right,
n turn left up steps, turn right at the top. The albergue is on the left.

ergue Los Blasones-Casagrande **PR** (42-4) r/Mayor 31 - ♦ 8€. Plus 4 rooms
15-30€. **K W D.** Bike storage. Bar next door does breakfast from 07.00. **X
v-Feb,** except for groups with reservation. Open from 11.00. ☎ 600 512 565.

ergue O Durmiñento **PR** (40) r/Mayor 44 - ♦ 10€. ◉ 10€. One room and
h for disabled. Leave by 09.00. Opens 11.00. **X Dec-Jan.** ☎ 982 531 099.

ergue dos Oito Marabedis **PR** (23÷7) r/Conde de Lemnos 23 - ♦ 9-10€. **K.**
en from 12.00. **X Nov-Apr.** ☎ 629 461 770.

ergue Don Alvaro **PR** (40÷4) r/Mayor 10 - ♦ 9€. **K,** with all facilities. **W @.**
en from 12.00. ☎ 982 531 592.

ergue-Cafetería International **PR** (38÷4) r/Mayor 57 - ♦ 10€. ◉ 9€. Bft
Separate M&F showers and WCs. **@.** Plus 2 rooms - ♦ ♦ 45€. **X Nov-Apr.**
982 535 109.

ergue A Pedra **PR** (23) Vigo de Sarria 19 - ♦ 10€. ◉ 9€. **K.** Plus 3 rooms -
♦ 45€. **X Dec-Feb.** ☎ 982 530 130. Next to the ⓘ on the way into town.

ergue Monasterio de la Magdalena (100÷5) av/de la Merced 60 - ♦ 10€. **K.**
en from 09.30. **X Nov-Easter.** ☎ 982 533 568.

ergue Alma do Camiño **PR** (100) c/Calvo Sotelo 199 - ♦ 9€. **W D K @.** ☎982
768. www.almadelcamino.com

ergue Barbacoa del Camino **PR** (18) c/Esqueiredos1 - ♦ 10€. **K W D @.** ☎
879 476. www.facebook.com/alberguebarbacoa

ergue Casa Peltre **PR** (22) Escalinata da Fonte 10 - ♦ 10€. **W D K @.** ☎ 606
067. www.casapeltre.es. Recently renovated house. Great sitting room.

ergue Credencial **PR** (28) c/do Peregrino 50 - ♦ 9€. **W D M @. Open all year.**
982 876 455. www.alberguecredencial.es

Albergue Casino **PR** (28) c/Mayor 65 - ♦ 10€. **K W D @.** ☎ 982 886 785. alberguecafeteriacasino@gmail.com

Albergue Casona de Sarria **PR** (31) c/San Lázaro 24 - ♦ 10€. **W D @. Open all year.** ☎ 982 535 556. www.lacasonadesarria.es

Albergue Matias **PR** (30) c/Mayor 4 - ♦ 9€. **W D @. Open all year.** ☎ 982 534 285. anuman43@hotmail.com. Next to great Italian restaurant. Don't miss the tiramisu!

Albergue Mayor **PR** (16) c/Mayor 64 - ♦ 10€. **W D K @.** ☎ 685 148 474. www.alberguemayor.com

Albergue Oasis **PR** (27) c/Vigo de Sarria 12 - ♦ 10€. **W D K @.** ☎ 982 535 516. www.albergueoasis.com

Obradoiro **PR** (38) c/Mayor 49 - ♦ 8€. **W D K @.** ☎ 982 532 442. arte-san@hotmail.es

Albergue Puente Ribeira **PR** (14) c/do Peregrino 23 - ♦ 9€. **W D M @.** ☎ 982 876 789. www.alberguepuenteribeira.com

San Lázaro **PR** (28) c/San Lázaro 7 - ♦ 10€. **W D K @.** ☎ 982 530 626. www.alberguesanlazaro.com

Albergue Los Blasones **PR** (42) r/Mayor 31 - ♦ 9€. **X Nov-Mar.** ☎ 600 512 565.

A&H *Albergue Granxa de Barreiros* **PR** (46) - ♦ 10€ ♦ 18€ ♦ ♦ 34€ Crta LU-633 km 54, ☎ 982 533 656 X **Nov - Mar** 4.5 kms outside of town offers free pickup from Sarria

H There are many hotels and hostels in Sarria. Some mentioned by pilgrims are:

Hostal Roma, c/Calvo Sotelo 2 - ♦ 50€. ♦ ♦ 60€. ☎ 982 532 211. www.hotelroma1930.es. | *Hospedaje Mar de La Plata* c/José Antonio - ♦ 40€. ♦ ♦ 58€. ☎ 982 530 724. www.hotelmardeplata.com. | *Hotel AlfonsoI X* Rúa do Peregrino 29 - ♦ 50€. ♦ ♦ 60€. ☎ 982 530 005. www.alfonsoix.com. | *Pensión O Camino* Calle Benigno Quiroga 16 - ♦ ♦ 50€. ☎ 626 205 172. | *Pensión Blasones* c/Ameneirizas 8 - ☎ 652 256 226. www.pensionblasones.es

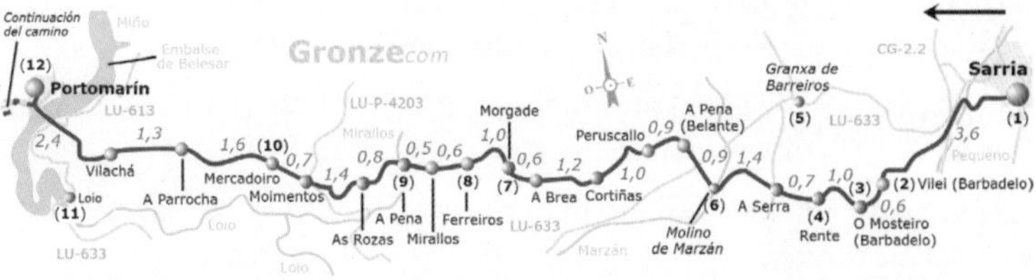

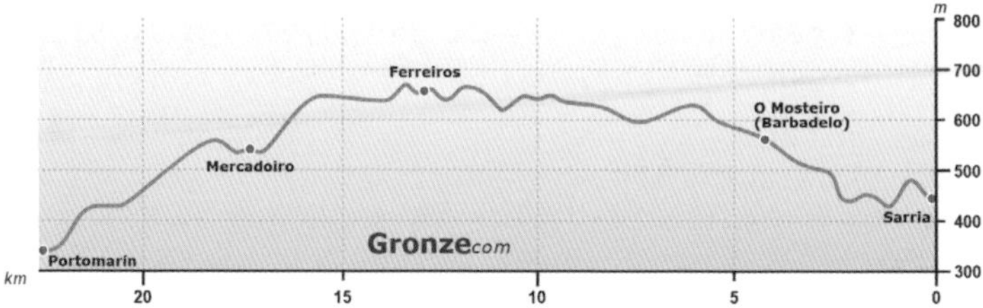

2.5 km to Vilei

A&H *Albergue Bar Restaurante Casa Barbadelo* **PR** (48÷6) - 🚹 9€. 🍽 9€. Bft 4.50€. **W D.** Plus 11 rooms - 🚹 🚹 45€. **X Nov-Feb.** ☎ 982 531 934. www.barbadelo.com

Albergue-Pension 108 to Santiago **PR** (14 + rooms) - 🚹 8-15€. **W D @.** Bft €. ☎ 634 894 524. pension108tosantiago@hotmail.com. www.pension108tosantiago.com

3.5 km to Marzan

A *Casa Albergue Molino de Marzan* (16) - 🚹 10€. 🍽 9€. Bft 5€. **W. X Mar-Oct.** ☎ 679 438 077. www.molinomarzan.com

4.5 Km to Barbadelo 115

A *Albergue Xunta de Galicia* (18) - 🚹 6€. **K,** without utensils. Often crowded. **Open all year.**

Albergue A Casa de Carmen **PR,** 100m after Xunta albergue (28) - 🚹 10€. **Meals. @.** ☎ 982 532 294. www.acasadecarmen.es

Albergue O Pombal **PR** (12÷1) - 🚶 9€. **K W D** 4€. Open 13.00-22.00. ☎ 686 718 732. Near the church in pink house, signed from the camino.

Albergue Molino de Marzán **PR** (16) Molino de Marzán Km 104.5 - 🚶 10€. **W D K @.** ☎ 679 438 077. www.molinomarzan.com

Casa Barbadelo **PR** (68) Vilei Km 108 - 🚶 9€. Meals. **W D @.** ☎ 982 531 934. www.barbadelo.com

H *Restaurante-Albergue Casa Carmen* (22-3) - 🚶 10€. 🍽 10€. Bft 5€. Plus 2 rooms - 🚶 🚶 35€, including breakfast. Open 13.00-22.00 ☎ 982 532 294. www.acasadecarmen.es

Casa Nova de Rente. 6 rooms - 🚶 25-28€. 🚶 🚶 30-38€. 🍽 10€. Bft 3.50€. ☎ 982 187 854. 150 m uphill to right of the albergue. www.casanovaderente.com. | *Casa Caxiguero.* 6 rooms - 🚶 44€. 🚶 🚶 55-66€. 🍽 16€ (organic). **X Christmas**. ☎ 618 951 344.

Hamlet with church dedicated to Santiago (open 15.00-18.00). Other bars and cafés along the route to Morgade.

7.5 km to Morgade 107

A&H *Bar-Pensión-Albergue Casa Morgade* **PR** (6÷1) - 🚶 10€. Plus 5 rooms - 🚶 🚶 28-35€. 🚶 supplement 12€. 🍽 8.50€. Bft incl. **X Dec-Feb.** ☎ 982 531 250.

1.5 km to Ferreiros 106

A *Albergue Xunta de Galicia* (22÷1) - 🚶 6€. **K,** without utensils. Warden runs bar *Casa Cruceiro* - 🍽 7-8€. Bocadillos, drinks and handicrafts.

Albergue-Restaurante-Bar Mesón Casa Cruceiro **PR** (16÷1) - 🚶 10€. 🍽 8-11€. Bft 3.50€. Plus 2 rooms - 🚶 🚶 40€. **X Dec-Feb.**

500m to Mirallos (650 m)

Bar/Rte O Mirallos

500m to A Pena

A&H *Casa do Rego* **PR** (6÷1) - 🚶 10€. Plus 2 rooms - 🚶 🚶 40€. 🍽 10€, poss bft incl. **W D @.** Bike store. ☎ 982 167 812. www.casadorego.com.

4.5 km to Mercadoiro

Albergue de Mercadoiro-Bar-Restaurant La Bodeguiña **PR** (32) - ♀ 12€. Plus 2 rooms - ♀ or ♀ ♀ 25-40€. ♦ 8.50-11.50€. Bft 3€. **X Oct-Mar.** ☎ 982 545 359. www.mercadoiro.com.

2 km to Vilacha

3 km to Portomarín (pop 2159 alt 324 m) 98

A new town, built when the old one was flooded by the waters of the new reservoir. The fortified Church of St Nicolás was dismantled stone by stone and rebuilt in its present town centre position. Plenty of shops, banks etc. Swimming possible. Go down the steps between the bridge and the youth hostal. Two bakeries specialise in almond *Tartas de Santiago*.

Río Miño from bridge

Church and Mass - *Iglesia de San Nicolás*, originally constructed 12th and 13th c. The portal is by Master Mateo, famous as the builder of the Pórtico de la Gloria of Santiago Cathedral. **Daily Mass 19.00 - followed by pilgrims' blessing.**

A *Albergue Xunta de Galicia* (110÷6) - ♦ 6€. **K,** without utensils. **Open all year.** Next to church in the town centre.

Albergue Ferramenteiro **PR** (130÷1) r/Chantada 3 - ♦ 10€. **K.** ☎ 982 545 362. www.albergueferramenteiro.com

Albergue Ultreia **PR** (14) c/Diputación 9 - ♦ 10€. **K.** Plus 5 rooms - ♦ ♦ 30€. ☎ 982 545 067. **Open all year.** www.ultreiaportomarin.com

Albergue Aqua **PR** (10) c/Barreiros 2 - ♦ 10€. **K W D @.** ☎ 608 921 372. www. aquarooms.es/index.php/en

Casa Cruz **PR** (16) c/Benigno Quiroga 16 - ♦ 10€. **W D @. Open all year.** ☎ 982 545 140. www.casacruzportomarin.com

Casa Marabillas **PR** (16) c/Monte 3 - ♦ 15€. **K W D @.** ☎ 744 450 425. www. casadomarabillas.com

Albergue Folgueira **PR** (32) avda/de Chantada 18 - ♦ 10€. **W D K @. Open all year.** ☎ 982 545 166. www.alberguefolgueira.com

Albergue Manuel **PR** (16) c/do Miño 1 - ♦ 10€. **W D K.** ☎ 982 545 385. www. pensionmanuel.com. *Albergue Novo Porto* **PR** (22) c/Benigno Quiroga 12 - ♦ 10€. **W D @.** ☎ 982 545 277. www.alberguenovoporto.com

Albergue Porto Santiago **PR** (14) c/Diputación 8 - ♦ 10€. **W D K @. Open all year.** ☎ 618 826 515. www.albergueportosantiago.com

Albergue Villamartín **PR** (20) c/do Peregrino 11 - ♦ 10€. **W D K @.** ☎ 982 545 054. www.alberguevillamartin.es

Albergue Pasiño a Pasiño (30) r/Compostela 25 - ♦ 10€. ☎ 665 667 243.

Albergue Pons Minea (24) av/Sarria 11 - ♦ 10€. ♦ 40€. ♦ ♦ 50€. ☎ 610 737 995.

A&H *Albergue-Pensión El Caminante* (12÷3) c/Benigno Quiroga - ♦ 10€. Bft 9€. Plus 15 rooms - ♦ 30€. ♦ ♦ 42€. **X Nov-Apr.** ☎ **982 547 575.** www.portomino.com

Albergue-Restaurant-Bar O Mirador **PR** (31÷6) c/Peregrino 27 - ♦ 10€. ⦿ 10€. Bft from 6.30. **Open all year**. ☎ 982 545 323. www.omiradorportomarin.com

H *Taberna Perez*, next to the *Guardia Civil* barracks at the top of the town, has accommodation up the lane - ♦ 34€, and a good *menú*. ☎ 982 545 040. | *Hostal Villa Jardín* (20÷2) r/do Peregrino 11 - ♦ 10€. Plus 36 rooms - ♦ 40-50€. ♦ ♦ 50-70€. ⦿ 12€. Bft. included. **X Nov-Apr.** ☎ 982 545 054. www.hotelvillajardin.com. | *Pension Mar* Rúa Fraga Iribarne - ♦ ♦ 40€. ☎ 622 611 211. | *Pousada de Portomarin* avda/Sarria s/n. The town's top hotel. Expensive. ☎ 982 545 200. www.pousadadeportomarin.es

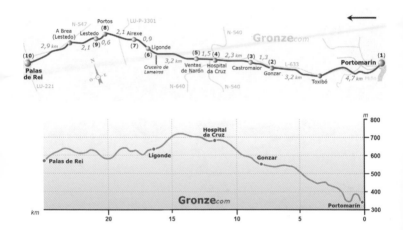

8 km to Gonzar 90

A *Albergue Xunta de Galicia* (28÷1) - ♦ 6€. **K. Open all year**. On main road at the far end of the village.

A&H *Albergue-Bar-Restaurant-Casa Garcia* **PR** (48÷2) - ♦ 10€. ⦿ 10€. Bft. Plus 4 rooms - ♦ ♦ 35€. **X Nov-Feb.** ☎ 982 157 842. At entrance to village.

1 km to Castromaior   89

A *Albergue Ortiz* **PR** (18) - ♦ 10€. **W D @.** Restaurant. ☎ 982 099 416, 625 668 991. info@albergueortiz.com. www.albergueortiz.com.

Café/Bar O Castro. Drinks, bocadillos, and 8€ *menú. Pension Maruja* has 4 rooms - ♦ 15-20€. ♦ ♦ 30-35€. ☎ 982 189 054.

2.6 km to Hospital de la Cruz 86

A *Albergue Xunta de Galicia* (30) - ♦ 6€. **K,** without utensils. **Open all year**. At far end of village (signed).

H *Hostal-Bar-Restaurante Labrador*. 9 rooms - ♦ 33€. ♦ ♦ 28.50-35€. ￥ 9€. Bft 3-4€. ☎ 982 545 303. Off to the left but visible from the camino. Has *sello*.

☞ There is the site of a pilgrim hospital on the right as you enter the village.

Pilgrim group

1.5 km to Ventas de Narón 84

2 bars. Plaza, rest area with *fuente*.

A *Albergue-Restaurante-Bar Casa Molar* **PR** (20) - ♦ 10€. 2 rooms - ♦ ♦ 30€. ￥ 9€. Bft, from 06.00 in summer. **Open all year**. ☎ 696 794 507.

Albergue O Cruciero **PR** (22÷2) - ♦ 10€. Also 2 rooms - ♦ ♦ 30-40€. ￥ 9.50€. Bft 3.50€. **X Dec-Feb.** ☎ 658 064 917.

3 km to Ligonde 81

A *Refugio Fuente de Peregrino* (10) - *Donativo*. 🍽 & Bft. Run by a religious organisation. **X Sept-May.**

Albergue Municipal Escuelas de Ligonde (20) - ⛺ 8€. **K W3€ D2€. X Dec-Apr.** ☎ 679 816 061.

H *Restaurante-Bar Casa Mari Luz. Menú* 9.50€. Closed in winter. Opens early, about 07.00, in summer.

1.5 km to Eirexe/Airexe 79

A *Albergue Xunta de Galicia* (30) - ⛺ 6€. **W D K. Open all year.**

A&H *Pensión-Albergue Eirexe* **PR** (6) - ⛺ 10€. 4 rooms - ⛺ 20-25€. ⛺ ⛺ 30-35€. **X Dec-Apr.** ☎ 982 153 475.

Bar-Restaurante Conde Waldemar. 🍽 10€. In a modern building opposite the albergue.

☞ **6 km detour to Vilar de Donas.** Take the lane on the right after **Portos** (not the path at km 71). The Church of *El Salvador* has 14th c. wall paintings and impressive effigies of Knights of the Order of Santiago, who settled here in 1184. Their role was not to protect pilgrims, although they did provide hospitals for them, but to protect Christian Spain against the Moors. Open Tues-Fri 10.00-15.00, Sat-Sun 13.00-19.00. Try house no 2 for key if the church is closed.

3.5 km to Portos/Lestedo

A *Albergue-Pensión A Paso de Formiga* **PR** (8) - ⛺ 10€. 🍽 10€. Plus 2 rooms - ⛺ ⛺ 40-50€.

Excellent municipal swimming pool is 1 km before Palas de Rei, just off the camino. Free. 1€ for compulsory *gorro* (cap).

4 km to Palas de Rei (pop 4500 alt 575 m) 72

Church and Mass - *Iglesia de San Tirso.* 12th c. **Daily Mass 19.00.**

A *Albergue Xunta de Galicia* (60÷5) - ⛺ 6€. **K,** no utensils. Laundry facilities. Drying area. Bike storage. Open 13.00-22.00. Leave 08.00. Good supermarkets very nearby.

Albergue-Bar-Restaurante Buen Camino **PR** (41) r/do Peregrino 3 - ☦ 10€. ▣ 9€. Bft 4€. **W D K.** Open 12.00. Leave 08.30. ☎ 982 380 233. Behind the Ayuntamiento.

Albergue Os Chacotes de la Xunta e Galicia (112÷3) - ☦ 6€. **K,** but no utensils. **W D. Open all year**. Open 13.00-22.00. At entry to town.

Albergue-Cafetería Mesón de Benito **PR** (78÷6) r/de Paz - ☦ 10€. ▣ 9€. Bft 2.50€. **W D. X Nov-Feb.** ☎ 982 103 386.

Albergue San Marcos **PR** (60) trav/de la Iglesia - ☦ 10€. Bft 4€. **K.** Plus 7 rooms - ☦ ☦ 50€. **X Jan-Feb.** ☎ 982 380 711.

Albergue Outeiro **PR** (50) pl/de Galicia 25 - ☦ 10€. **W D K @.** ☎ 982 380 242, 630 134 357. info@albergueouteiro.com. www.albergueouteiro.com

Albergue Castro **PR** (56÷9) av/de Ourense 24 - ☦ 10€. **W D K @.** ☎ 982 380 321, 609 080 655. info@alberguecastro.com. www.alberguecastro.com

Albergue A Casiña de Marcello **PR** (17÷2) camiño/da Aldeia de Abaixo - ☦ 10€. **W D K @.** ☎ 640 723 903. albergueacasina@gmail.com. www.albergueacasina.es

H *Pensión Palas de Rei* 2 c/Santirso. www.pensionpalas.es. | *Casa Curro*, avda/ Ourense 15, first on left in first main road as you enter town. ☎ 982 380 044. Good food. Bft from 08.00. | *Hospedaje Guntina* plaza/del Ayuntamiento - ☦ 15€. ☎ 982 380 080. | *Hostal Vilarino* avda/Compostela 16, close to the Xunta albergue. ☎ 982 380 152. | *Hotel Casa Benilde* c/Mercado s/n - ☦ 42€. Bft 5€ (not on Sunday). ☎ 982 380 717. www.hotelcasabenilde.com. | *Hostal Rte Ponterroxan,* 500 m out of town on left - ☦ 30€. ☎ 982 380 132. www. hostalponteroxan.es.

Bar round the corner from the *Xunta* albergue will do a simple meal at any time. Rooms next door at *Café Bar Plaza.* ☎ 982 380 109.

Buy food here if you are planning to stay at the Xunta albergue in Casanova.

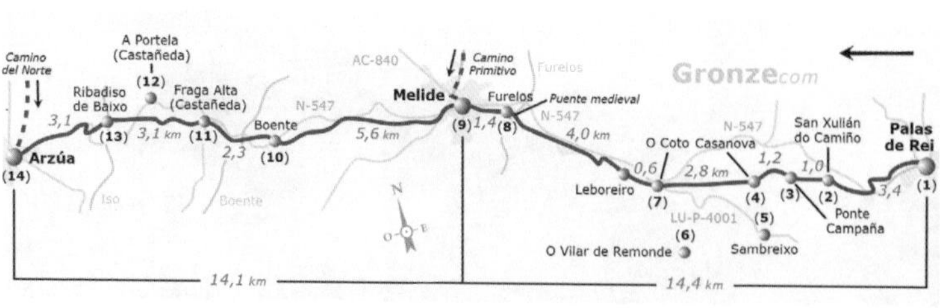

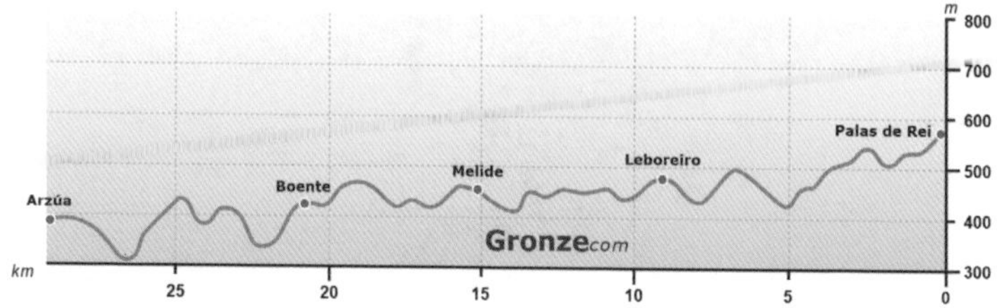

3 km to San Xulián 69

A *Albergue O Abrigadoiro* **PR** (18) - 🚹 10-12€. 🍽 10€. Bft 3.50€. **X Nov-Mar.** ☎ 982 374 117. A delightful stopping place. www.abrigadoiro.es.tl.

2 km to Ponte Campana 67

A *Albergue Casa Domingo-Taberna* **PR** (18÷2) - 🚹 10-12€. Plus 3 rooms - 🚹 28€. 🚹 🚹 36-40€. 🍽 10€. Bft 3.50€. **X Oct-Apr.** ☎ 982 163 226.

1 km to Casanova (alt 480 m) 66

A *Albergue Xunta de Galicia* (20) - 🚹 6€. **K,** without utensils. **Open all Year.** ☎ 982 173 483. Key (and *sello)* from Carmen at house on left before albergue.

Albergue A Bolboreta **PR** (8) - 🚹 13€. 🍽 9€. Bft included. Plus 8 rooms, all en suite - 🚹 35€. 🚹 🚹 42€. About 2 km off the camino (signed). Possible to stay more than 1 night. ☎ 609 124 717.

Between Casanova and Leboreiro you enter the Galician province of A Coruña - the seventh and last province on the camino.

Hórreo (old Galician grain store), San Xulián

3.5 km to Leboreiro (alt 440 m) 62

H (in nearby O Coto) *Hostal Rural-Bar-Restaurante de los Somoza*. 10 rooms - ♦ 47€. ♦ ♦ 55€. ⦿ 18€. Bft 6-8.50€, from 07.00. **X Dec-Feb**. Essential to phone in advance. ☎ 981 507 372. www.casadelossomoza.es

☞ Church of Santa Maria has a Romanesque tympanum.

4 km to Furelos

H *Bar Farrugo - Taberna do Farrico*.

☞ Roman Bridge, Church of San Juan, *sello* available.

2 km to Melide (pop 8000 alt 460 m) 56

An important small market town with several churches: *San Roque* on right at the entry to the town. *Santa María* on western outskirts. Key available nearby. *Sancti Spiritus*, the parish church is in the town centre. *Sello* available 17.00-19.00.

Church and Mass - *The Iglesia Sancti Spiritus was formerly a Franciscan monastery in the 14th c. On the main altar there is a magnificent baroque altar piece by created by Francisco de Castro Canseco in the 17th c. He also sculpted the impressive altarpiece of the Church of San Paio in Santiago.* **Daily Mass 19.15.**

A *Albergue Xunta de Galicia* (156÷7) r/San Antonio - **†** 6€. **K**, without utensils. **W D**. Bike storage. Stables. Near the Church of Santa María in r/San Antonio. Key from number 23. *Albergue Alfonso II El Casto* **PR** c/Toques y Friol 52 (35) - **†** 10€. **K W D @.** ☎ 981 506 454. www.alberguealfonsoelcasto.com

Albergue Melide **PR** (42) avda/Lugo 92 - **†** 10€. **W D @.** ☎ 981 507 491. www.alberguemelide.com

Albergue O Apalpador **PR** (30) c/San Antonio 23 - **†** 10€. **W D K @. Open all year.** ☎ 981 506 266. www.albergueoapalpador.com

O Apalpador **PR** (24) canton/de San Roque 9 - **†** 10€. **W D K @. Open all year.** ☎ 981 506 266. www.albergueoapalpador.com

Albergue O Cruceiro **PR** (72) ronda/de A Coruña 2 - **†** 10€. **W D K @.** ☎ 616 764 896. www.albergueocruceiro.es

Albergue Pereiro **PR** (45) c/Progreso 43 - **†** 10€. **W D K @. Open all year.** ☎ 981 506 314. www.alberguepereiro.com

Albergue San Antón **PR** (36) c/San Anton 6 - **†** 10€. **W D K @.** ☎ 981 506 427. www.alberguesananton.com

Albergue Vilela **PR** (24) c/San Antón 2 - **†** 10€. **W D K @. Open all year.** ☎ 616 011 375. calberguevilela@gmail.com

Albergue Arraigos **PR** (20) canton/San Roque 9 - **†** 10€. **Open All Year.** ☎ 646 941 887. albergue.arraigos@gmail.com. www.alberguearraigos.com

Albergue Montoto **PR** (40) r/Codeseira 31 - **†** 10€. ☎ 646 941 887. alberguemontoto@gmail.com. www.alberguemontoto.com

H *Hotel Restaurante Carlos* avda/de Lugo 119. 33 rooms - **†** 25-35€. **† †** 35-50€. ⦿ 10€. Bft 6€. ☎ 981 507 633. Opp Peugeot Garage on main road. www.hc96.com

Hotel-Pensión-Restaurante Xaniero 1 avda/de la Habana & Rúa San Pedro 22. Hotel, 26 rooms - ♦ 35€. ♦ 45€. Pensión, 11 rooms - ♦ 30-40€. ☎ 981 505 015. www. hotelxaneiro.com. | *Pensión-Restaurant-Bar El Molino* r/Rosalía de Castro 15. 12 rooms - ♦ 25€. ♦ 25-35€. ⏺8.50€. Bft 2.50€. ☎981506048. | *PensiónBerenguela*, r/de San Roque 2 - ♦ 30€. ♦ 40€. ☎ 981 505 417. www.pensionberenguela.com. There is no shop in Ribadiso de Baixo, so if you intend to cook there buy food here.

Melide is famous for pulpo *(octopus) a Galcian speciality. To try it at its best go to* Casa/Pulpería Ezequiel, *a traditional* Pulpería *serving spiced octopus in wine on wooden platters with bread and that other delight of Galicia, white Ribeiro Wine.* Casa Ezequiel *is on the left hand side of the main road shortly before the main square.*

6 km to Boente (alt 400 m) 50

A *Albergue-Bar Os Albergues* **PR** *(30)* - ♦ 10€. ⏺ 10€. Bft included. **W D. X Dec-Feb.** ☎ 981 501 853.

Albergue-Bar Boente **PR** *(28÷5)* - ♦ 11€. ⏺ 9€. Swimming pool. **X Dec-Feb.** ☎ 981 501 974.

Albergue El Aleman **PR** *(40÷4)* - ♦ 12€. **W D @.** Restaurant. ☎ 981 501 984. info@albergueelaleman.com. www.albergueelaleman.com.

Bar Bareta. Opens 08.00 in summer, later out of season. Bocadillos and other snacks.

Church of Santiago - very pilgrim friendly. *Sello* is offered.

From O Cebreiro to here the camino has been very largely downhill following river valleys. From here on it crosses numerous small river valleys. This involves many ups and downs.

2 km to Castañeda 48

H *Pension-Albergue-Bar Santiago.* 2 rooms - ♦ ♦ 30€. ⏺ 9€. Bft 3€. **W D.** ☎ 699 761 698. | *Casa Pazo de Sedor.* 11 rooms - ♦ 44-55€. ♦ 58.40-73€ ⏺ 17.50€. Bft 6€. ☎ 981 501 600. Leave camino by continuing through village & uphill to right. Café Bar *No Camino* on right at the edge of the village.

3.5 km to Ribadiso do Baixo 45

A *Albergue Xunta de Galicia* (70÷4) - 🚹 6€. **K,** without utensils. Open 13.00-22.00. Leave by 08.00. In converted pilgrim hospital in a scenic position by a river.

Albergue Los Caminantes 1 **PR** (56) - 🚹 8-10€. **K W D. X Mar-Nov.** ☎ 981 500 295.

Albergue Milpes Ribadiso 7 **PR** (24) - 🚹 10€. **W D K @. Open all year.** ☎ 981 500 425.

H *Bar-Restaurante Mesón Rural Ribadiso* - 🍽 9€. Just past the Albergue.

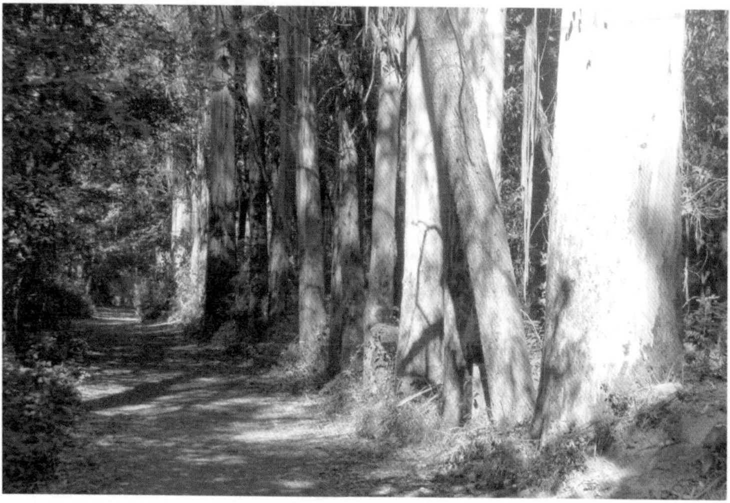

Path to Arzúa

3 km to Arzúa (pop 6934 alt 389 m) 42

Church and Mass - *Iglesia de Santiago.* **Daily Mass 19.00.**

A *Albergue Xunta de Galicia* (46) c/Cima do Lugar - 🚹 6€. **K,** with no utensils. Open 13.00-22.00. Leave by 09.00. **Open all year.** ☎ 981 500 455. Near Santiago church, just left off the main street.

Albergue Vía Lactea (120÷8) c/José Antonio 26 - 👤 10€. Bft 3.50€. **W D.** ☎ 981 500 581. Off to the left of the camino after the Xunta albergue

Albergue da Fonte (20) r/do Carmen 18 - 👤 10-12€. **K.** ☎ 659 999 496.

Albergue Ultreia (31) avda/de Lugo - 👤 10€. 🍽 7-10€. Bft 3€. **W D. X Dec-Feb.** ☎ 981 500 471.

Albergue Don Quijote/Pensión Rúa (50÷3) c/Lugo 130 - 👤 10€. Plus 19 rooms - 👤 35€. 👤 👤 45€. 🍽 9€. Bft 2.50€. ☎ 981 500 139.

Albergue Los Caminantes (26) Carretera Santiago 14 - 👤 8-10€. **K W D.** Open 11.00-22.00. **X Mar-Nov**. ☎ 647 020 600.

Albergue Turístico Santiago Apóstol (84) avda/de Lugo 107 - 👤 10-12€. 🍽 9€. Bft 2.50€. **K W D. Open all year**. ☎ 981 508 132/981 500 004.

Albergue A Conda **PR** (18) c/Calexa 92 - 👤 10€. **W D K @.** ☎ 981 500 068. www.pensionvilarino.com

Albergue Arzúa **PR** (20) c/Rosalía de Castro 2 - 👤 10€. **W D K @.** ☎ 981 508 233. www.pensionarzua@gmail.com

Albergue De Camino **PR** (46) c/de Lugo 118 - 👤 10€. **W D K @.** ☎ 981 500 415. www.decaminoalbergue.com

Albergue De Selmo **PR** (50) c/de Lugo 133 - 👤 10€. **W D K @.** ☎ 981 939 018. www.oalberguedeselmo.com

H *Casa Frade*, Rúa de Ramón Franco - 👤 30€. Old fashioned, family run. ☎ 981 500 019. www.casafrade.arzuacomercial.com. | *Hospedaje Carballeira,* next to Casa Frade, has rooms and group accommodation. ☎ 981 500 094. www.casacarballeira.com. | *Meson do Peregrino* at r/de Ramon Franco 7 is pilgrim friendly with good food and 5 👤 👤 rooms. ☎ 981 500 145. www.mesondoperegrino.com. | *Hostal O'Retiro,* opposite a garage on the way into town has nice rooms - 👤 30€. 👤 25€ without bath. ☎ 981 500 554. | *Pensión Rúa*, on left entering town, a white 4-storey building - press the buzzer. ☎ 696 162 695. www.pensionrua.com. | *Hostal Casa Teodora* c/de Lugo 38 - 👤 24€. 👤 👤 45€. 🍽 10€. ☎ 981 500 083. www.casateodora.com

☞ Arzua is famous for its cheeses. Shops, wide choice of bars and restaurants in the main part of town

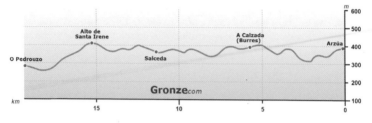

8 km to A Calle

Bar Lino. Open for breakfast 2.50€. *Menú de la Casa* 8€.

Tia Dolores serves drinks, snacks and bocadillos. Accommodation may be available.

3 km to Salceda (alt 360 m) 29

Albergue de Boni **PR** (25) - ♊ 12€. **W @. ☎** 618 965 907. N547, just past the green house. www.facebook.com/albergueboni

A&H *Albergue-Turístico-Hostal-Restaurante Salceda* **PR** (8) - ♊ 10-12€. 🍽 9.50€. Bft 4-6€. Plus 14 rooms - ♊ 30€. ♊ ♊ 45€. **☎** 981 502 767. www.albergueturisticosalceda.com

Albergue Alborada **PR** (10) - ♊ 12€ . ♊ ♊ 50 €. **X Nov-Mar. ☎** 981 502 956.

H *Mesón A Esquipa* - 🍽 8.50-12€. Mixed reports. 3 bars. *Taberna Salceda* at entrance to the village.

⇨ **After Salceda the camino leaves the road again.**

Camino Francés 2018/19

3 km to Empalme 26

H *O Ceadoiro* serves a good cheap meal, 9€. You can order in advance as you pass on your way to the albergue at Santa Irene, then go back uphill later to eat it (not Sundays). The restaurant/bar on the other side of the N547, *Mesón O Empalme,* also has a reasonably priced menu.

⇨ **Arrows here point both downhill along the main road and to the right for a path through the forest (safer and more pleasant). The forest path has a well-signed left turn leading to the private albergue via a subway under the road. Continue straight ahead to rejoin the main road and Santa Irene Xunta de Galicia albergue.**

1.5 km to Santa Irene (alt 380 m) 24

A *Xunta* (36) 300 m downhill from the crossroads - ♦ €6. Kitchen is poorly equipped. Quieter at the back for sleeping. Open 13.00.

Albergue Rural Astrar **PR** (24) Astrar 18, 700m from the camino - ♦ 10€. **W D K @. Open all year.** ☎ 981 511 463. www.alberguerruralastrar.com

Albergue Santa Irene **PR** (15) - ♦ 13€. Bft. **W D.** ☎ 981 511 000.

2 km to A Rúa 22

H *Hostal/Rte O'Pino* A Rúa 9 - ♦ 27-38€. ♦ ♦ 40-50€. Pleasant. Good reports on *menu del día*, 12€. Clean. Used by groups. Tends to get crowded. May be closed on Sundays. ☎ 981 511 148. | *Casa do Acivro* - rooms 45€. *Menu del dia* 13-20€.

⇨ To go to Pedrouzo/Arca look out for painted arrows pointing to the left as the camino crosses a major road before entering a forest.

Sign near Salceda

1.5 km to Pedrouzo/Arca 21

Church and Mass - *Iglesia de Santa Eulalia.* **Daily Pilgrims' Mass at 19.30.**

A *Albergue de la Xunta de Galicia* (120÷4) - ♣ €6. **K,** with some utensils. **Open all year**. On left opposite 1st *farmacia*, on right behind *Correos*.

Albergue Porta de Santiago **PR** (54÷13) avda/de Lugo 11 - ♣ 10€. **NK W D.** Bar/restaurant opposite has a good 11€ menu. **X Jan-Feb.** ☎ 981 511 103. On Rt on the main road past the Xunta albergue, shortly before some local government buildings. www.portadesantiago.com

Albergue Edreira **PR** (48÷4) La Fuente 19 - ♣ 10€. **W D. X Nov-Feb.** ☎ 981 511 365. www.albergue-edreira.com

Albergue O Burgo (14) avda/de Lugo 47 - ♣ 10€. **W D.** Plus 5 rooms - ♣ ♣ 35-40€. **X Nov-Mar.** ☎ 981 511 406. www.albergueoburgo.es

Albergue Cruceiro de Pedrouzo (94) avda/de la Iglesia 7 - ♣ 10€. Bft 4.50€. ♠ 10.50€. **K W D @.** ☎ 981 518 204. www.alberguecruceirodepedrouzo.com

Albergue Otero **PR** (36) c/de Forcarei 2 - ✝ 10€. **W D @.** ☎ 671 663 374. www.albergueotero.com

REMhostel **PR** (50) avda/de la Iglesia 7 - ✝ 10€. **W D @.** ☎ 981 510 407. www.alberguerem.com

H *Pensión Maruja* r/Nova 9. 6 rooms - 30-40€. ☎ 630 404 138. | *Pensión Arca* Rúa Os Mollados 25. 7 rooms - ✝ 30-36€. ✝ ✝ 35-45€. ☎ 657 888 594/981511437. | *Pensión Maribel* Pedrouzo, next door. 7 rooms - ✝ 40€. ✝ 45€. | *Casal de Calma-Casa Rural-Cafetería* Lugar da Igreixa. 8 rooms - ✝ 40€. ✝ ✝ 45-50€. |◉| 10€. Bft 4€. **Open all year.** ☎ 680 910 676. | *Hostal En Ruta SCQ* avda/de Santiago 23 - ✝ 25€. ✝ ✝ 35€. ☎ 981 511 471. www.enrutascq.es. | *Pensión O Pedrouzo* avda/Santiago 13 - ☎ 671 663 375. www.pensionpedrouzo.com. | *PR Una Estrella Dorada* - ✝ 35€. ☎ 630 018 363. | *Pensión 9 de Abril* avda/Santiago - ✝ 40€. ✝ ✝ ✝ 60€. ☎ 606 764 762. www.pension9deabril. com. | *Pensión A Solaina* Pedrouzo - ✝ 40€. ✝ ✝ ✝ 60€. ☎ 633 530 918. www. pensionasolaina.com. | *Pensión Condesal* r/Codesal 17 - ☎ 981 511 061. www.pensioncodesal.com.

A village in a eucalyptus forest. Shops, including a *supermercado* and *cafetería*, next to the *Xunta* albergue. Bars, bank and health centre.

⇨ *To rejoin the* camino *take the main road to the* Casa do Concello. *Turn up the road by the side of the building to rejoin the camino near a school on the edge of the forest. Alternatively, backtrack east to join the* camino *where it crosses the main road.*

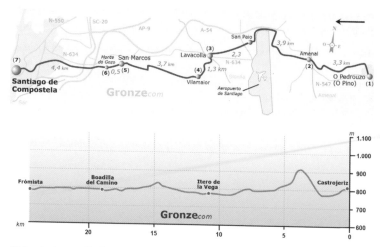

10 km to Lavacolla (alt 300 m) 11

A *Albergue Lavacolla* **PR** (34) c/Lavacolla 35 - ✝ 12€. **W D K @.** ☎ 981 897 274.

H *Hostal La Concha.* 12 rooms - ✝ ✝ 30-45€. ◉ 10€. Bft 5€. ☎ 981 888 390. | *Hostal San Paio.* 45 rooms - ✝ 27-40€. ✝ ✝ 39-50€. ◉ 10€. Bft 3.50€. ☎ 981 888 205. *Hotel Garcas.* 30 rooms - ✝ 31.50-35€. ✝ ✝ 45-50€. ◉ 10€. Bft 5€. ☎ 981 888 225. www.hotelgarcas.com. | *Hotel Ruta Jacobeo.* 20 rooms - ✝ ✝ 50-70€. Bft 8.50€. ◉ 14.50€. ☎ 981 888 211. www.rjacobea.com/hotel.

In earlier times Lavacolla was the traditional washing and purification place for pilgrims before they entered Santiago.

6 km to Monte de Gozo 4.5

Also known as *Monxoi* or "Mount Joy", and Chapel of *San Marcos.* Celebrated as the first point from which the towers of the Cathedral were visible and so a place of great joy and celebration for pilgrims down the centuries. It is now hard to see the towers of the Cathedral from here, because of the trees which have grown in the middle distance. Until it was developed by the Xunta de Galicia for Holy Year 1993 it was a tranquil green hill.

⇨ To get to the albergue here follow the signs and arrows to the top of the hill, then continue down for c. 500 m. It is on the left, well signposted.

A *Albergue de la Xunta de Galicia-Cafetería del Complejo*. Call ahead out of season. This albergue has about 400 places in dormitories. The charge is 6€ per night. There are kitchens and facilities for washing and drying clothes are available. Open from 19.00-22.00. **Open all year**. The cafetería has a 10€ menu, and serves sandwiches and hot dishes.

Albergue Parroquial (40) c/das Estelas - *Donativo*. **D K W**. ☎ 981 597 222. Run by the local parish which is staffed by Polish priests. www.albergue.pl (in Polish).

4.5 km to Santiago de Compostela (pop 105,851 alt 264 m)

You arrive first in the suburb of San Lázaro, which has a chapel on the site of a former leper Hospital. ⓘ kiosk (summer only) has street maps of Santiago. Although you are now in Santiago de Compostela, it will take you at least another three quarters of an hour to reach your ultimate destination, the Cathedral in the old quarter.

⇨ The pilgrim way to the Cathedral (see map p 150)

As you walk down from Monte de Gozo be aware that soon you will encounter the first albergues - they are all signed. If you have chosen an albergue or reserved a place you may wish to ensure that you don't pass it on the way into Santiago only to have to walk back out again. Also, these days the Cathedral does not allow admission to pilgrims with rucksacks, so you may care to check into your albergue before walking into the centre. After the chapel of San Lázaro, the pilgrim route is via c/de los Concheiros, r/San Pedro, Cruz de Homo Santo (a calvary), Puerto del Camino, Casa Reales, Plaza de Cervantes, c/Azabachería, Plaza de Inmaculada (aka Azabachería), then straight on and down a flight of steps under the arch. Turn left into the main square in front of the Cathedral, the Plaza del Obradoiro.

A handy map of Santiago follows. For a full list of all albergues, hostels, hotels and things to do please use the CSJ's booklet: Pilgrim Guide to Santiago de Compostela.

Cathedral of Santiago de Compostela

Camino Francés 2018/19

SANTIAGO DE COMPOSTELA

Calle de las Trampas,
leading to the Seminario
Menor de Belvis (refuge)

CONCHEIROS

150